Songs

without

Words

Songs *without* Words

The Art

of the

Paperweight—

Rick Ayotte

by Lawrence H. Selman

The artist wishes to acknowledge the genius of John T. Hogan, who fabricated many of Ayotte's special glassworking tools.

Special thanks to the following collectors who donated pieces for this book:

Jean Backman, Minnie C. Bolster, Wayne Eaton, Henry Fuller, Gem Antiques, Frederick and Barbara Lane, Rutherford/Joubert Collection, Lois Sandler, D. C. Smith, Mark Smith, Emile Tetu, L. H. Selman Ltd. and various other anonymous lenders.

Special thanks to the following photographers for lending photos for this book:
K. S. Brooks Photography and Steven Hope.

Head of Production/Editor: Ronald Rosenberg
Photographer: Mary Ann Hauck
Designer: Gideon Amparo, Jr.
Proofreader: Stephanie Clark

Front cover: A252: Breath of Life, A200: Red Salamander in Marsh, A292: Blueberry Hill, A63: Marsh Wren with Nest.
Back cover: A145: Eastern Meadowlark with Black-Eyed Susans, A81: Seascape, A210: Apple Magnum, A76: Keel-Billed Toucan.

For more information about paperweights and the International Paperweight Society please contact L. H. Selman Ltd.

INQUIRIES
L. H. SELMAN LTD.
761 Chestnut Street
Santa Cruz, CA 95060
800 538–0766
408 427–1177

Library of Congress Catalog Card Number: 96-070312
ISBN: 0–933756–23–2
Printed in Hong Kong

Contents

A81: Ocean Scene

Artist Appreciation

by Paul Stankard

Through dedication and discipline Rick Ayotte has mastered his craft and works creatively in a unique way, expressing his love of nature through vibrant color and personal vision. Rick is not only a master paperweight maker, but he brings a colorist's instinct to his nature art, inspired by his beloved New Hampshire woods.

I met and became friends with Rick Ayotte in 1963, when we were both working as glassblowers for Macalaster Scientific in Nashua, New Hampshire. We started our careers in glass at the same time, and now, when I look back over thirty-three years of shared friendship, paperweight and wildlife experiences, it feels special to have Rick as a steadfast friend.

The most meaningful aspect of our friendship is the memories we share vacationing with our families at the South Jersey shore, swimming and fishing in Maine, and the occasional weekend spent trout fishing in the New Hampshire wilderness. I remember the early days and Rick's passion for glass and wildlife, and now, able to look back over three decades, it is obvious how he has become an acknowledged American master in the art of the paperweight. The dedication that Rick Ayotte brings to glass has earned him the respect of his contemporaries and hundreds of paperweight enthusiasts who see and share in Rick Ayotte's work a celebration of beauty.

A1: Male Cardinal

The Discovery of Nature Through the Eyes of an Artist

by Jan Smith,

Curator of The Bergstrom-Mahler Museum, Neenah, Wisconsin

I was first introduced to the work of Rick Ayotte through an example in the collection of The Bergstrom-Mahler Museum. The work was a small, single, red cardinal in a clear casement. Its realistic portrayal seemed rather specimen-like as it perched frozen in its glass enclosure.

It seemed curious to me that anyone would attempt the subject matter of birds in an art form that held strongly to decorative principles. In a genre dominated by floral themes and millefiori patterns, the glass equivalent of *wildlife art* seemed a daring attempt at personal preference in a market that was historically indifferent and unprepared for change. Acknowledging a few reptiles, amphibians and butterflies, fauna rarely served as a source of inspiration in nineteenth-century glass paperweights.

I have since come to realize that Ayotte's work was probably defined somewhat by one of those unusual twists of fate and somewhat by a personal determination to pursue his love of nature through the medium of glass.

Under the encouragement of friend and veteran paperweight artist Paul Stankard, Ayotte's debut in 1978 offered the paperweight world a new cadre of ideas. His early works brought forth the cardinal and the goldfinch, soon to be followed by the woodthrush, the purple finch, scarlet tanager, bluebirds, robins and a covey of feathered specimens to entice the armchair ornithologist. Ayotte's following grew as his mastery of techniques increased his ability to create a realistic portrayal of birds.

From 1979 to 1984, he worked to not only increase the species represented in his work, but to refine his lampwork skills. Representation of numerous pieces within the confines of a clear glass dome appeared to be an effortless task for Ayotte, although the opposite situation is more accurate. Each new work required careful experimentation and often the acceptance of many losses before arriving at success. As my familiarity with his work increased, I realized his motivation was not necessarily market driven, but played through an inner song that repeated its harmonious refrain.

Ayotte listened closely to a melody that echoed reminiscences of countless childhood hours spent freely exploring the woods and studying animals. Sometimes the melody trilled like the lyrical sounds of a cardinal perched high in a tree, and sometimes it thundered like a cacophony of sea gulls circling above the shore. However, it is that song and his enthusiasm for wildlife that is replayed with each new design.

The earliest works were tenuous. The medium of lampworking requires a careful balance of skill, color sense and composition. The paperweights of the nineteenth century, so inspiring to today's artists, generally took great liberty with detail in floral themes to offer a colorful, fanciful object. Ayotte's ambition was to create works that exhibited a careful attention to detail to portray a convincing subject. In striving for an accurate rendering, Ayotte could not rely on his childhood memories alone, but returned to careful observation of his subjects in their natural habitat when possible or methodical research in photographs.

*Opposite:
The first works
were tenuous;
Mouse (1977),
Sea Turtle
(1977), and
Crab (1976).*

Ayotte's birds gained a more naturalistic appearance and coloration. As the birds became more complex, their environments also needed to increase in complexity. Therefore, in the early years of his work, there is an interesting fluctuation between the development of a new bird form and development of a habitat, until the skill and repertoire of each piece in a scene was mastered to combine them with ease.

*Detail of
A94: Blue
Jay Near
Stream*

In the early 1980s, Ayotte began working towards a means of using colored glass rod as a painter might use a paint brush to apply color selectively. This technique allowed for a more naturalistic blending of colors to achieve a more gradually shaded area and a smoother transition from one color to the next. He created a series of *Glasscapes*—

paintings created from colored glass rod encased in clear domes. The first works using this effective method were *Ocean Scene* (1981), with a sea gull in flight over a rolling ocean, and *Blue Jay Near Stream* (1982), in which a blue jay perches on a branch with a stream flowing behind it. These were the first works identified as Glasscapes, however, a one-of-a-kind piece created in 1980 seems to initiate the idea. It is a masterful depiction of a house wren on a branch with a softly glowing sun placed behind it. The Glasscapes continue to be a significant departure from paperweight traditions.

Detail of A232: Family of Ducks on a Pond

Ayotte also attempted upright three-dimensional compositions in the mid 1980s. His first was a bird, and then a frog that could be viewed in an upright position from all sides, rather than showing the profile commonly used in paperweights. There were an inordinate amount of variables to control and pitfalls to avoid in these pieces.

In 1984, he began experimenting with scenes that simulated water in a pond. By 1986, Ayotte produced his first successful upright bird in a paperweight. By the following year, he had created two successful designs with upright motifs. The research necessary to create new work is costly and time consuming in a medium such as glass. It requires tremendous determination.

The study and development for producing the Glasscapes and the upright works, no doubt led to the extraordinary dimensional work Ayotte has produced since 1986, such as the frog and salamander weights which depict a complex natural habitat. In this work, Ayotte changed the viewer's perspective from the traditional approach. The dimensionality of these works set them apart from other Ayotte designs.

In *Family of Ducks on a Pond* (1991), a culmination of many of the previous ideas, the overall viewing area is still a topical one, but the depiction is such that it suggests the viewer is privy to a glimpse of a full, lush, natural habitat. The composition extends to the sides rather than emphasizing a central placement. In this way, the view suggests a segment of life as it happens, not necessarily prearranged. In this ambitious work, Ayotte is able to showcase his versatility.

Detail of A265: Walden Pond

Detail of A242:
American Beauty
Red Rose Bouquet

In *Family of Ducks on a Pond* (1991) or *Walden Pond* (1994), an equally ambitious and dimensional portrayal of turtles gliding effortlessly through the water, the artist examines the tranquil life at the water's edge that he so closely identified with as a child. In these works, he is clearly able to unify a true passion and an inquisitive sense of nature with the skill developed through his creative endeavors in glass. This unification of natural image with imagination is the culmination of explorations summoned from his childhood and artistic expression.

In Ayotte's traditionally presented work, decorative qualities prevailed. By looking into a piece from the top, the viewer saw a profile of a bird placed in a carefully arranged vignette of foliage or flowers, designed to enhance or support the circular composition with the bird as the central image. Beginning in 1984, Ayotte started to combine more highly developed floral specimens with his birds. He used a compound technique of layering the composition to create depth and complexity in his imagery.

Many of the more decorative paperweights build on the nineteenth-century paperweight tradition. These works are appealing because of Ayotte's ability to create a realistic rendering of naturally beautiful flower forms. In such works as the *Pink Peace* (1991) and the *American Beauty Red Rose Bouquet* (1992), Ayotte captures one of the most perfect flowers in glass with elegance and grace.

By 1991, Ayotte was creating elaborate floral bouquet forms without birds in the composition. He introduced a series of upright works called Illusions, which enhanced the interior composition with cutting and color. These works were faceted around the edges and had a circle of

Detail of
A230: Pink Peace

translucent colored glass at the back that emitted a soft halo of color around the central composition. Faceting and colored grounds were techniques that enhanced paperweights of the nineteenth century. This decorative effect offered a more contemporary approach, and showcased the skill and versatility the artist has built since the early cardinal of 1978.

The floral language of nineteenth-century paperweights was built on equal parts of whimsy, illusion and romanticism. There was only a remote reference to naturalism. There is a much stronger emphasis in works of the twentieth century, however, to rely heavily on botanical accuracy and naturalistic detail to achieve success, and to a somewhat lesser degree, flamboyance.

The paperweight of the twentieth century, as we have come to know it, is characterized by "breakthroughs" or discoveries of virtuoso technique, new ideas, more detail, new formats, and the exploration of exotic subject matter. Ayotte's work embodies the demands and challenges the art form faces as we close another century.

As artists like Ayotte strive to continually improve their work, their concerns are not only for meeting the needs of changing tastes, but also for meeting the challenges of creating work that will be pivotal in the paperweight arena and carry the art form forward to a position of significance in the twenty-first century.

Ayotte is among those artists who are not often satisfied with what they create. They continue to confront themselves, question their efforts and evaluate their work by a set of profound personal standards. As an artist, he is among those who are excited by facing challenges and striving to create new, significant work that can only be judged by the test of time.

A278: Paradise

Inspirations

by Rick Ayotte

hen I consider my youth in New Hampshire, I am always amazed by the many unimaginable adventures I embarked on, as well as the fact that I am still alive. I was one of the "jump first and look later" variety of children, and my activity levels tended to exceed what was allowed inside the confines of enclosed structures. From an early age, I ventured out into the world where I found an inexhaustible fascination with the large woodlands, fields and rivers that surrounded my home.

I think it was during this time that I learned what an adventure it was to be outdoors. This period permanently impacted my artistry, and I thought that by perhaps sharing some of my adventures people might better understand the excitement I find in nature, that I try to put into each paperweight. As an artist, I have worked in relative isolation and it is my childhood and the flavor of my world that has most greatly influenced my paperweights.

On one instance I found myself walking down the railroad track with my dog Skippy. While journeying along the tracks he came across what I imagine was a powerful scent and began digging furiously in the ground. I recall standing there with a curious fascination, which quickly turned to alarm when Skippy pulled a four-foot snake out of the ground. I hurriedly grabbed a plastic bag laying nearby and stuck the snake in the bag. Fortunately, or so I thought at the time, the next day happened to be Halloween. I took advantage of this ideal opportunity to pester a bad-tempered neighbor that lived close to my home. That night I placed the bag on the front steps to her home and rang the doorbell. I watched from a bush in the perfect position as she opened the bag and terror struck. Her loud scream was the only thing that covered my laughter on that occasion.

I do remember boasting to a few of my friends about my accomplishments. Strangely this story was not only told between friends, but the next day it appeared on the radio and in the newspaper. For a young boy such as myself suddenly to be elevated to celebrity status was a sheer joy. This woman raised quite a stink as she told of the prank. The small town syndrome, I suppose.

The artist, five years old with sisters Connie & Theresa.

Most of my childhood experience was not as censurable as this one and most of my time was spent taking pleasure in the astonishing flight of birds, metamorphosing tadpoles, elusive salamanders and endless forms of plant life. At times, perhaps because of my age, I held the desire to capture these things, and so I carved slingshots and bows and arrows, feeling like a warrior of the earth, but catching no more than the wondrous sights that would eventually inspire my paperweights.

My fascination with animals always seemed to lead to trouble. On one occasion, I only hoped to give my neighbor assistance, but nature held other intentions. At this time I was around eleven or twelve years old enjoying a summer evening. My friend and I were poking around and we happened to see a skunk run across the street. We pursued it to see where it would go, and while we were chasing the skunk, it ran under a neighbor's porch. Being the kind young men that we were, we knocked on the door and waited for the owner to come out. When we informed the house's owner of the whereabouts of the skunk, he started to search under the porch steps. After he removed a few boards and dug a few peep holes, we joined him in the mad search. Finally we'd removed every step on his porch. Disheartened, we were unable to "skunk" out the skunk, my friend and I stood up, and as we did, it ran right past us and sprayed the owner. Already you are beginning to see why I was not one of the most popular children in the neighborhood.

Age thirteen, one of the youngest Eagle Scouts in Troop 257.

Hampton Beach, NH, 1957. Ayotte proudly displays a pair of cod caught with his bare hands.

My time in the outdoors has left me with a number of memories that are sheer magic. On one particular occasion, I recall walking with my friend through a swamp near my house. He was a little ahead of me at the time when I noticed within the stream what appeared to be a giant fish. I swore to him it must have been a pickerel at least five feet long. He rushed back to see the fish.

As he did, I threw my wooden spear into the water hoping to catch this beauty. Of course I was not successful, and, as he came near, the fish slowly wiggled into the depths. As expected, he called me a liar and laughed out loud at the idea of such a large fish. However, a week or so later we were in the same area and a blue jay was flying across the water. All of a sudden this giant fish came out of the water and grabbed the blue jay. Well, needless to say, my friend instantly believed not only in me but also in Jonah!

You still may not believe this story, but I grew up during an era when it was possible to witness such rare sights. The streams were teeming with life, and after much thought I've decided the fish must have been a pike or a muskie that reached the swamp through an offshoot of the Merrimack river.

To this day, when I am not making paperweights you'll find me ice fishing on Golden Pond or birdwatching in the wilderness surrounding my home. I'm proud to participate in the tradition of American wildlife artists in this country, sharing my vision of the world through the unique medium of glass. My goal has always been to interpret nature with a fresh eye; to share the drama I see all around me. Most importantly, I want to remind others of their own stories by telling them some of mine.

Taking time out from work, secret fishing spot in the White Mountains.

Florida, 1982. Playing with the sea gulls, while the rest of the family visits DisneyWorld.

18

A134: *Monarch Butterfly with Wood Sorrel*

Pioneering Wildlife in Glass

by Lawrence H. Selman

On a trip to the New York World Fair in 1964, Rick Ayotte spotted some paperweight making tools sitting on a glassworker's workbench. His first exposure to the art form left him incredulous that someone would spend their time making objects to hold down paper.

Ayotte talks about how perplexed he felt: "I asked him, 'What are those things?' and he told me they were paperweight making tools. I said, 'Who in the world would waste their time making paperweights?'"

Today, of course, Rick Ayotte is one of the most highly esteemed paperweight makers in the world. It was the outrageous notion that someone could spend their life making paperweights that piqued his curiosity, and began his journey along a path that would permanently impact the history of glass.

My first encounter with Rick Ayotte happened in 1978 at the famed Corning Museum of Glass exhibit known today as The Great Paperweight Show. It seemed unusual to me that a young man could be so totally immersed in his art. There was a passion that showed in his words and his glasswork. Today, Ayotte remains one of the most dedicated and prolific artists I have known, often working twelve hours a day, six and seven days a week.

His story begins with a rise to success from humble beginnings. It's a tale one might read in a Horatio Alger novel. As the oldest male of seven children, it fell on Ayotte's shoulders to take care of his family when his father died. At age 18, with few employment prospects, he started working as a truck driver at Macalaster Scientific Glass Company in Nashua, New Hampshire. During his lunch hour he became a regular visitor to the lampwork area, where he watched, mesmerized, as glassworkers created scientific glass equipment. The glassworkers befriended Ayotte. Eventually they began teaching the excited teenager the rudiments of lampworking and allowing him to experiment with the equipment. His aptitude for lampwork became apparent, and after working at the company for only four months, he was promoted from his trucking job to apprentice in the glass shop.

After working in the glass shop for five years, Ayotte started his own business, *Ayotte's Artistry in Glass*. He began by creating crystal lampwork animals which were sold at the San Diego Zoo, on the Queen Elizabeth II cruise ship and other gift stores across the United States. When Paul Stankard showed Ayotte his botanical paperweights in 1977, he was immediately enthralled.

"I liked the idea that you were looking into another world," he says. "There was something pleasing and intimate about the spherical shape of paperweights that really appealed to me. It opened a lot of doors for me artistically."

Ayotte's artistry begins with his passion for nature, especially the flora and fauna surrounding his New Hampshire home. He is a master woodsman who possesses an extraordinary amount of knowledge about plants and animals. His interest in the outdoors started in childhood. Recapturing images and feelings from childhood is a theme that runs throughout his work. Many pieces are filled with a childlike wonder.

"I used to get up early in the morning and walk around the woods every day before school," he says. "It's still hard to describe how it made me feel. I watched birds, squirrels, beavers, plants, insects—everything. I was learning, but it felt like an adventure. I try to instill that feeling in my work, the same excitement I felt as a young man."

Childhood was a time of adventure for Ayotte, and many of his experiences growing up in rural New Hampshire are reminiscent of *Huckleberry Finn*. On one occasion, he took a dresser drawer and sailed it across the Merrimack river. On another, he was boxed into a corner by a 100-pound turtle in bad temper. After a fierce struggle, he ended up donating the turtle, which weighed about the same as he did, to a neighborhood mother's soup pot.

Detail of
A302: Carribean Night

Ayotte's special fascination lies with birds, a fact that has delighted armchair ornithologists around the world. As a youth, he charted migratory bird groups, studied their feeding patterns and carved life-size birds out of wood. It was only natural that the first paperweight design he created would contain a bird. During his career he has translated over 80 different species of birds into glass, creating over 300 different designs.

"My whole life I've had an enthusiasm for getting close to wild things," he says. "I translate those observations into the scenes I create in paperweights. For example, one thing I've found is that every bird has a distinct personality. A wren is perky and I try to show that through its pose and bearing. An eagle, on the other hand, has a majestic demeanor. When you capture that special energy in a piece, it really comes to life."

He possesses an ability to interact with wildlife like no other person I've met. He can call out to a cardinal in a tree and the bird will descend down onto his head. By making a little titter, he easily coaxes a chipmunk into his lap. With the right call, he draws deer and moose to the edge of the woods by his home. Ayotte regularly interacts with many of the birds portrayed in his work, and it is not unusual for him to spend days studying a particular creature of interest. A number of the birds he portrays—blue jays, phoebes, mockingbirds, doves, redpolls and chickadees—are a regular part of his forays into the woods.

"I call myself a glass naturalist or a wildlife artist," says Ayotte. "My work is a vehicle that allows me to share the qualities of nature with people who have little exposure to it. I've found an understanding of the wonders of our world leads to a more responsible treatment and a respect for our natural environment."

Detail of A212: Fall Bouquet Plaque

For Ayotte it is as important to portray a mallard duck's coloring as it is to capture the feeling one gets watching it swim in a pond. Each piece contains accurate detail, but Ayotte also imparts a special sense of romance to each scene—the evidence of his utopian vision of nature. The familiar way animals react to Ayotte perhaps accounts for the fairy-tale atmosphere that appears in many of the scenes he creates.

While many see him as a wildlife artist, his work is just as validly viewed from the standpoint of colorist. The use of color, in combination with motifs Ayotte chooses to portray, stimulates the senses on an instinctual animal level. Ayotte's most simply defined artistic goal perhaps best defines the intent of his work "to create a little world in a sea of color."

Careful scrutiny of each work reveals the intelligent application of color to share emotion and establish atmosphere. The angry lines of a peregrine falcon threaten the viewer from a cold blue ground, instilling the design with the predatory fierceness of the bird. The soft petals of the roses in his effective *Pink Peace* (1991) are accented with pastel blue green leaves that heighten the sense of peace and tranquillity in the otherworldly, serene design.

In his Illusion series, Ayotte applies his refined knowledge of glass optics to create a halo of color around his internal imagery. To create this effect he places a spot of color in the back of a rounded plaque. The curvature of the glass diffuses the color around the design. This innovative coloring technique, whose double does not exist in painting, helps set the mood of his designs. A ruby halo instills his *Fall Bouquet Plaque* (1990) with a warm pastoral grandeur. The golden halo surrounding his *Crab Apple Bouquet Plaque* (1991) colors the design with an Indian summer warmth.

Detail of A225: Crab Apple Bouquet Plaque

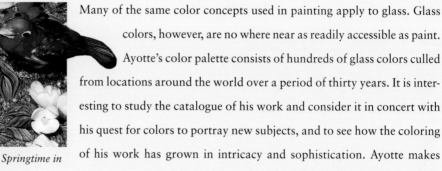

Detail of A160: Springtime in New Hampshire

Many of the same color concepts used in painting apply to glass. Glass colors, however, are no where near as readily accessible as paint. Ayotte's color palette consists of hundreds of glass colors culled from locations around the world over a period of thirty years. It is interesting to study the catalogue of his work and consider it in concert with his quest for colors to portray new subjects, and to see how the coloring of his work has grown in intricacy and sophistication. Ayotte makes special use of his varied palette in such works as *Midnight Blue* (1996), a seascape that makes use of numerous shades of blue to create a panoramic view of a rolling ocean. Ayotte's color palette, in concert with the sophisticated Glasscape technique, is applied to create a remarkable sense of depth in a four-inch diameter design.

Ayotte conceives each design with the intent of encasing it in a crystal shell. This overlooked aspect of his artistry is integral to the magic of his work. It's only when the imagery is placed underneath the glass dome that it really comes to life. The changes wrought through encasing a design with molten crystal are astounding. The hot touch of the crystal transforms the glossy texture of his lampwork

Rare & magnificent, Cardinal Window (1991)

pieces into soft feathers, delicate flower petals and ripe berries. A sudden magnification of the imagery discloses detail that was only previously apparent to the artist.

Over the years Ayotte has successfully explored many different encasement formats, producing most notably bowls, cylinders, cubes and some rare and magnificent windows, but he always seems to return to the traditional paperweight dome.

While later works display a maturity and sophistication that goes beyond his first works, there is something thrilling about the early pieces. They are "firsts" created by an artist daring to test the limits of glass. They mark the triumphant steps of an artist into new ground, carrying with them a vibrant aura brought on by the joy of discovery. Among the many times Ayotte has interpreted cardinals, no clear favorite emerges. Each masterpiece resounds with the strength that comes when an artist attempts to share his soul through an art medium. As one who has been familiar with Ayotte's work for more than twenty-five years, I've seen this involvement recognized by an extraordinary number of collectors who must own each example of butterfly, parrot or rose.

Ayotte's quest to create worlds is most fully realized in three-dimensional scenes of amazing intricacy that were introduced in the late eighties, beginning with the revolutionary *Springtime in New Hampshire* (1986). These pieces, which are meant to be viewed from all angles like Paul Stankard's Botanical series, are the culmination of a desire that has guided Ayotte's work from the outset—the desire to tell a story with his imagery. Surrounded by three-dimensional scenery, his wildlife portrayals take on a startling life. The viewer is transported to each time and place. The eerie red eyes of a loon glow behind the vegetation of a pond bank overgrown with blueberries and wildflowers. A pond slider turtle prepares to surface through the pond foam next to a vibrant lily. To fully appreciate the intricacies of these works requires careful study. They are the electrifying masterpieces of an artist in his prime.

In contrast to more static paperweight designs, Ayotte's weights are characterized by action. Hummingbirds furiously beat their wings as they search for nectar in fuchsia blossoms. A spider tenses to snatch an unsuspecting fly from a flower blossom. Irate nestlings peep hungrily below a bluebird with a worm in its beak. Ayotte captures an instant of time that sums up the entire experience.

Ayotte is, incidentally, one of few artists to have collaborated with Paul Stankard, an honor that springs from their lifelong friendship and mutual admiration. These rare designs have always been highly coveted.

"Living in the woods of New Hampshire, Rick Ayotte has dedicated his life to the art of the paperweight. His mastery of glass and his consummate familiarity with nature have brought a fresh vocabulary to the art form," says Stankard.

A portion of Ayotte's power lies in his ability to continually transcend the boundaries of what was thought possible with glass. There is something fabulous about these pieces created by a man who has abandoned the words of critics and deliberately chosen to work apart from the influence of other artists, relying solely on the voice of nature and his unique experience for inspiration. It was with great pleasure I watched his talent recognized when he received the International Paperweight Society Award for Excellence in 1996. Each of Ayotte's designs is a visual poem locked in crystal, a celebration of art and nature that will move the spirit of art lovers and serve as the study pieces of rising artists for centuries to come.

First annual International Paperweight Society Award for Excellence presented to Rick Ayotte at the 1996 IPS Festival.

A245: Amazon Parrots Magnum Plaque

A Comprehensive Record

of the

Artist's Work

1978-1996

Each edition is shown in the year when it was initially created; several editions were produced over consecutive years and may be dated with the later year. No two pieces in an Ayotte edition are ever exactly alike, and one will discover many special details in any particular piece. Ayotte's traditional paperweights are created in three basic sizes; standard measuring approximately 3 1/2 inches, miniature measuring approximately 2 1/8 inches and magnum measuring above 4 inches. The Illusion plaques generally stand 4 inches tall; triple weights average 6 inches in height.

Each description includes the designated number of pieces for each edition, including figures for standard, miniature, and magnum when applicable. Some of the editions were not completed. Each piece is signed and dated by the artist. Text in italic are notes from the artist.

We were unable to obtain photos of five rare pieces (A20, A61, A142, A186, and A250). Descriptions for these missing pieces are provided in Items Missing from the Record on page 151.

1978

A1. MALE CARDINAL

A bright red cardinal perches self-importantly on a branch. Produced in faceted and unfaceted crystal. Limited edition of 50.

This was the first edition I produced. Even though I'd already been working as a lampworker for fifteen years, it felt like starting over. The piece was very well received. Paul Jokelson, the quintessential connoisseur of birds in paperweights, saw the piece and refused to believe the cardinal was made out of glass. "It must be ceramic," he said.

A2. MALE WOOD THRUSH

A male wood thrush balances on a wooden stilt. Produced on clear or opaque green ground, in faceted and unfaceted crystal. Limited edition of 50.

I always admire this migratory bird when I see it in the woods. It has an especially beautiful song.

Detail of A301: Misty Blue

A3. MALE & FEMALE CARDINAL

Ayotte records the differences between male and female cardinals. Produced in faceted and unfaceted crystal. Limited edition of 25.

This was the first double bird weight I created. It was a major step towards portraying a more inclusive vision of nature. I have always been fascinated with the interaction of animals and this was the first step towards capturing it in glass. It was also rewarding to document the male and female of a species. There are many interesting comparisons between these two birds.

A4. OPEN-WING WOOD THRUSH

A brown and white wood thrush soars gracefully through the sky. Limited edition of 50.

This was the first open-wing bird design I created. By portraying the bird in action, I took another step towards animating the glass.

A5. MALE GOLDFINCH

A male goldfinch billows its feathers on a bare branch. Produced in faceted and unfaceted crystal. Limited edition of 50.

A little yellow jewel that I often saw as I walked through the fields when I was young.

A6. MALE & FEMALE GOLDFINCH

A pair of goldfinches play a bashful courting game atop a leafy branch. Produced in faceted and unfaceted crystal. Limited edition of 25.

A7. FEMALE GOLDFINCH

A female goldfinch perches on a curved branch in this rare design. Produced in faceted and unfaceted crystal. Limited edition of 5.

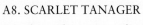

A8. SCARLET TANAGER

A male scarlet tanager clings to a bare branch. Limited edition of 50.

A9. MALE SCARLET TANAGER

A male scarlet tanager watches a caterpillar crawl over a leaf. Produced in faceted and unfaceted crystal. Limited edition of 50.

These birds frequently nested near my grandfather's barn when I was growing up.

A10. MALE & FEMALE SCARLET TANAGER

A male and female tanager look curiously at a caterpillar in the branches of a tree. Produced in faceted and unfaceted crystal. Limited edition of 25.

A11. SCARLET TANAGER IN FLIGHT

Ayotte revels in the brilliant colors of a scarlet tanager in flight. Limited edition of 25.

A12. GOLDFINCH & SCARLET TANAGER

A wily scarlet tanager eyes a yellow feathered goldfinch in the branches of a tree. Limited edition of 50.

A13. FEMALE SCARLET TANAGER

A female scarlet tanager patiently waits for a suitor atop a leafy branch. Produced in faceted and unfaceted crystal. Limited edition of 5.

A14. EASTERN BLUEBIRDS

A male and female bluebird frolic in leafy branches. Produced in faceted and unfaceted crystal. Limited edition of 50.

One of my favorite birds. A common sight throughout my life that once was a great harbinger of spring. My spirits still soar when I see one.

A15. SINGING BLUEBIRD COMPOUND

A bluebird sings in leafy branches that have been layered to create a sense of depth. Limited edition of 50.

A16. EASTERN BLUEBIRD IN FLIGHT

An eastern bluebird spreads beautiful blue wings. Limited edition of 3.

A17. ROBIN ON BRANCH

A robin perches cheerily on a tree branch. Produced in faceted and unfaceted crystal. Limited edition of 50.

This is another bird that has always been exciting to me because of its announcement of spring.

A18. MOTHER ROBIN WITH BABY

A mother robin attends to a crying chick. Produced in faceted and unfaceted crystal. Limited edition of 25.

This was my first weight to include baby birds—a compelling design element.

A19. DOWNY WOODPECKER

A downy woodpecker prepares to eat a red worm on a branch. Produced in faceted and unfaceted crystal. Limited edition of 50.

A21. MALE TOWHEE

A male towhee eyes a scrumptious black and white bug. Produced in faceted and unfaceted crystal. Limited edition of 3.

A22. BLACK-CAP CHICKADEE

A black-cap chickadee nestles among pine cones and fragrant green pine needles. Produced on clear or sky blue ground, in faceted and unfaceted crystal. Limited edition of 50.

A23. FEMALE CARDINAL

A female cardinal poses on a leafy green branch. Produced in faceted and unfaceted crystal. Limited edition of 5.

A24. MALE CARDINAL IN FLIGHT

A male cardinal races skyward to his nest. Produced in faceted and unfaceted crystal. Limited edition of 25.

A25. CALIFORNIA QUAIL

A California quail searches for food. Limited edition of 25.

A26. YELLOW-THROATED WARBLER

A yellow-throated warbler balances on top of green marsh reeds. Produced in faceted and unfaceted crystal. Limited edition of 50.

I have vivid memories of standing waist high in water and being eaten by mosquitoes while observing this bird.

A27. YELLOW-THROATED WARBLERS IN REEDS

A male and female warbler rest atop green marsh reeds. Produced in faceted and unfaceted crystal. Limited edition of 25.

A28. BALTIMORE ORIOLE

The intricate markings of an oriole are portrayed with superb accuracy. Produced in faceted and unfaceted crystal. Limited edition of 50.

On rare occasions I have been fortunate enough to bear witness to this bird's striking color. Early in my life this influenced my level of intrigue with birds.

A29. MALE BALTIMORE ORIOLE WITH NEST

A Baltimore oriole protects its nest in an oak tree. Limited edition of 25.

A30. SPARROW HAWK

A sparrow hawk is portrayed with talons spread to catch prey. Limited edition of 50.

I have observed this hawk many times hovering like a helicopter over prey.

Detail of A185: Blueberry Bouquet

1980

A31. EASTERN BLUEBIRDS COMPOUND

A male and female bluebird court on a leafy branch. Limited edition of 50.

I was very excited to discover how much depth I could create by placing lampwork at different levels in the glass. The compound technique helped me to further create the feeling that one was looking at these birds in the woods.

A32. PURPLE FINCH ON SNOW

A purple finch greets the morning from a snowy branch. Limited edition of 50.

The dramatic reddish-purple color of this winter bird of northern New Hampshire against the snow gave me the opportunity to create a cozy winter scene. This weight is part of the collection of The Corning Museum of Glass and The Currier Museum in New Hampshire.

A33. PEREGRINE FALCON ON BLUE

A peregrine falcon surveys the world from the upper branches of a tree. Limited edition of 50.

It caught my interest because it is one of the fastest birds in the world. A few rare pieces show a mountain in the background.

A34. BLACKBURNIAN WARBLER ON PINE NEEDLES

A yellow-headed blackburnian warbler takes shelter in a cluster of green pine needles. Limited edition of 50.

A35. BLUE & GOLD MACAW

First in the Tropical Bird series. A blue and gold macaw chatters from a branch of green jungle leaves on an opaque green ground. Limited edition of 50.

The colors and the size of this bird prompted me to choose it as my first tropical design.

A36. MALE & FEMALE MACAW PARROTS

Second in the Tropical Bird series. A pair of blue and gold macaws swing from side to side on jungle branches. Limited edition of 25.

A37. REDHEADED WOODPECKER

A redheaded woodpecker hammers on an oak tree with a hollow and golden acorns. Limited edition of 50.

A38. WOODPECKERS WITH CLOUDS COMPOUND

A pair of woodpeckers chisel away at a tree trunk in front of a cloud-filled sky. Limited edition of 50.

A39. DOWNY WOODPECKER WITH RACCOON

The pecking of a downy woodpecker awakens a cozy raccoon from its nap in the hollow of a tree. Limited edition of 25.

A40. HAWK OWL

First in the Bird of Prey series. A hawk owl stares ominously from a branch. Limited edition of 75.

My first owl design. I tried to capture the unnerving stare of this nighttime hunter.

A41. HAWK OWL WITH MOON

Second in the Bird of Prey series. A hawk owl looks curiously around under a full, yellow moon. This piece was produced on a black or purple ground. Limited edition of 50.

A42. HAWK OWL DOUBLE COMPOUND

Third in the Bird of Prey series. A pair of hawk owls commune under the night sky. Produced in faceted and unfaceted crystal. Limited edition of 25.

A43. HERRING SEA GULL

A herring sea gull hops over a log. This piece was created on a clear or blue ground, in faceted and unfaceted crystal. Limited edition of 75.

I have enjoyed the ocean throughout my life and spent much time watching and feeding the gulls. There was little doubt whether I would attempt to create this bird.

A44. HERRING SEA GULL IN FLIGHT

A herring sea gull dives through a blue, cloud-filled sky. Faceted and non-faceted. Limited edition of 25.

A45. HERRING SEA GULL & SANDPIPER

A herring sea gull cautiously watches a sandpiper on an opaque black ground. One-of-a-kind.

A46. HERRING SEA GULLS COMPOUND

Gulls circle a herring sea gull perched on a branch. Limited edition of 25.

A47. REDHEADED WOODPECKER IN OAK TREE

A redheaded woodpecker clings to an oak tree with a fledgling peeping from a hollow. Limited edition of 25.

A48. REDHEADED WOODPECKERS

A woodpecker watches over a nesting baby which pokes its head out of a hollow in a tree. Limited edition of 25.

A49. MALLARD DUCK WITH CATTAILS

A male mallard parades along the length of a marsh log with cattails. Produced on clear or sky blue ground. Limited edition of 50.

The iridescent green head attracts many to this duck, especially children. I vividly recall proudly watching my children feed these ducks at local ponds.

A50. MALLARD DUCK FEMALE

A female mallard duck marches along a log by reeds. Limited edition of 50.

A51. MALLARD DUCK ON A POND COMPOUND

A mallard duck glides over a blue pond with cattails. Faceted. Limited edition of 50.

A52. MALLARD DUCK IN FLIGHT

A mallard heads south for the winter in a cloud-filled sky. Limited edition of 25.

A53. WESTERN MEADOWLARK

A western meadowlark poises its head curiously on a log with grass. Limited edition of 50.

A54. WESTERN MEADOWLARK WITH RAINBOW

A western meadowlark sings cheerfully under a beautiful morning rainbow. Limited edition of 50.

This is a bird of open fields and in my mind I pictured it singing after a rain storm in a field with a rainbow bending to its voice.

A55. CRISSEL THRASHER

A crissel thrasher pauses on a branch in a cluster of golden yew leaves. Limited edition of 50.

A56. GREAT WHITE HERON ON A LOG

A great white heron poses on a log. Produced on opaque green or blue ground. Limited edition of 50.

At the turn of the century these graceful birds were massacred when plume hunters killed them to use their plumes for women's hats.

A57. GREAT WHITE HERON COMPOUND

A great white heron ambles over a log in a pond before an audience of flying herons. Limited edition of 25.

A58. GREAT WHITE HERON & FROG

A great white heron wades through a blue pond with lily pads in pursuit of a green frog. Limited edition of 50.

A59. HOUSE WREN

A house wren peers curiously from a leafy tree branch. Limited edition of 50.

With its perky attitude and swift flight, the wren monopolizes many of our bird houses.

A60. HOUSE WREN WITH SUN

A house wren warms itself on a leafy tree branch in the sunshine. One-of-a-kind.

A62. BLUEBIRD & GOLDFINCH

A bluebird and a goldfinch peer alertly around a leafy branch. Limited edition of 50.

A63. MARSH WREN WITH NEST

A long-billed marsh wren watches protectively over a nest hidden in dense reeds on an opaque green ground. Limited edition of 25.

A64. SULPHUR-CRESTED COCKATOO

Third in the Tropical Bird series. A sulphur-crested cockatoo preens on a branch with tropical leaves over a blue ground. Limited edition of 50.

This is the white and golden-crested cockatoo of the South American jungles.

A65. SULPHUR-CRESTED COCKATOOS COMPOUND

Fourth in the Tropical Bird series. Two sulphur-crested cockatoos rendezvous on a tropical jungle branch. Limited edition of 25.

A66. BALTIMORE ORIOLE WITH ACORNS COMPOUND

A Baltimore oriole hops to the end of an oak branch with acorns. Limited edition of 25.

A67. ROSE-BREASTED GROSBEAKS

A pair of rose-breasted grosbeaks sing contentedly in an oak tree with a nest. Limited edition of 15.

In my younger years I can recall walking aimlessly through the woods only to be startled by the powerful and melodious song of the grosbeak.

A68. ROSE-BREASTED GROSBEAK WITH FLEDGLINGS

A rose-breasted grosbeak watches over three peeping chicks in a nest. Limited edition of 25.

A69. ROSE-BREASTED GROSBEAK FEMALE

A female grosbeak hops along a branch in an oak tree. Limited edition of 5.

A70. ROSE-BREASTED GROSBEAK MALE

A male grosbeak rests in an oak tree. Limited edition of 50.

A71. MUTE SWAN

A mute swan drifts serenely over a glassy pond. Produced in faceted and unfaceted crystal.

I have always admired its grace and beauty. The swift lines of the neck challenged my artistic ability.

A72. YELLOW-BILLED CUCKOO

A yellow-billed cuckoo looks for dinner in a webbed nest of gypsy moth caterpillars. Limited edition of 50.

I sketched this bird while driving to the White Mountains, when my family and I stopped alongside the road to cook some recently caught trout.

A73. YELLOW-BILLED CUCKOOS

Male and female cuckoos perch on a branch near the beginnings of a nest. Limited edition of 25.

A74. WOOD THRUSH WITH OAK LEAVES

A wood thrush prepares to fly from an oak tree on an opaque green ground. Limited edition of 50.

A75. MALE & FEMALE WOOD THRUSH

A pair of wood thrushes court on an oak branch. Limited edition of 50.

A76. KEEL-BILLED TOUCAN

Fifth in the Tropical Bird series. A keel-billed toucan dozes on a jungle branch. Limited edition of 50. Miniature—unlimited.

A colorful South American bird that captured my imagination because of its vibrant colors and beak.

A77. KEEL-BILLED TOUCAN COMPOUND

Sixth in the Tropical Bird series. A pair of toucans socialize on a lush tree limb. Limited edition of 25.

A78. THE GREAT FLAMINGO WITH PALM TREE COMPOUND

Seventh in the Tropical Bird series. A great flamingo wades in water by an island with a palm tree and a flying flamingo on a sky blue ground. Limited edition of 50.

A79. PAINTED BUNTING

A painted bunting swings from a branch with leaves and blue berries. Limited edition of 50.

A80. ROBIN WITH THREE CHICKS

A robin holds an earthworm above three crying fledglings in a nest. Limited edition of 25.

This was the first time I integrated a nest into a design.

A81. OCEAN SCENE

First in the Glasscape series. Sea gulls circle the cliffs by a rolling ocean. Limited edition of 25.

A unique form of painting on glass similar to how an artist paints on canvas. The glass, heated in the torch, becomes liquid just like a paint. This is the first of my glass paintings.

A82. BROWN THRASHER IN POISON SUMAC LEAVES

A brown thrasher peers alertly from a grove of poison sumac. Limited edition of 50.

I spent a day raptly watching these birds eat berries on my uncle Jerry's farm.

A83. EASTERN PHOEBE WITH GRAPES AND FOLIAGE

An eastern phoebe dozes on a vine bearing ripening grapes and foliage.

This is a voracious insect eater with a song that sounds exactly like its name. I heard my first phoebe at Boy Scout Camp, early in the morning as I worked on my bird study merit badge.

A84. CHESTNUT-SIDED WARBLER

A chestnut-sided warbler perches in brilliant fall foliage. Limited edition of 50.

This is one of the most active consumers of leaf-eating insects that lives along the edges of woodlands.

A85. DICKCISSEL WITH PINE CONES

A yellow-throated dickcissel peers timidly from a pine thicket. Limited edition of 50.

I positioned this bird in one of its nesting areas, the pine groves, where it can blend into the landscape.

A86. BARN SWALLOW WITH BUG

A barn swallow swoops down to grab a bug crawling on a reed in a gathering of cattails. Limited edition of 50.

I spent many days mesmerized by these agile insect eaters as they scurried to gather their prey, flying back and forth from my grandfather's barn.

A87. BARN SWALLOW

A barn swallow flies away from a field of cattails. Limited edition of 50.

A88. WHITE-CROWN SPARROW

A white-crown sparrow contemplates the world from a golden yew branch.

This seed eating bird visits many backyards in North America, especially those with freshly sown grass seed.

A89. WESTERN TANAGER

A western tanager cocks its head curiously at the viewer from green branches. Limited edition of 50.

This handsome bird has an amazing ability to project its voice with a ventriloquial quality and is often found among the treetops along the forest edge.

A90. WESTERN TANAGER IN FALL FOLIAGE

A western tanager chirps a cheerful song to an audience of fall leaves. One-of-a-kind.

A91. CAROLINA CHICKADEE

A Carolina chickadee gingerly inches out to the end of a pine branch. Limited edition of 50.

A92. DANCING UNICORNS

A pair of unicorns dance above a rainbow on an opaque yellow ground. One-of-a-kind.

Detail of A127: Golden-Back Oriole with Nest & Babies

1982

A93. BLUE JAY

A blue jay screeches in a thicket of chokeberries. Limited edition of 75.

While attempting to walk through the woods silently, it is often the blue jay that gives away my position. This is a colorful but pesky bird that frequently positions itself outside the windows of my shop.

A94. BLUE JAY NEAR STREAM

Second in the Glasscape series. A blue jay perched on a stem of chokeberries prepares to splash in a flowing stream. Limited edition of 25.

A95. HOUSE SPARROWS

A pair of house sparrows mingle in leafy tree boughs. Produced on amber or gray ground. Limited edition of 50.

As a young boy I watched them flit around the house. They nested in our gutters. For many years now they have taken lodging outside my daughter's bedroom window.

A96. WHITE-CROWN SPARROW WITH ROSE

A white-crown sparrow hops over to a blushing pink wild rose in this collaboration with Paul Stankard. One-of-a-kind.

A97. SPARROW

A sparrow looks inquisitively at a bursting seed pod on a wild arum flower in this collaboration with Paul Stankard. Five and one faceting. One-of-a-kind.

A98. BLACK-CAP CHICKADEE WITH WOOD SORREL CUBE

A black-cap chickadee searches for insects in the ground beneath a blooming wood sorrel plant in this collaboration with Paul Stankard. One-of-a-kind.

A99. CHICKADEE WITH PINE CONES COMPOUND

A black-cap chickadee perches in a tuft of pine needles above a pine cone. Limited edition of 25.

We often feed this family favorite sunflower seeds from the palm of our hands.

A100. YELLOW-THROATED VIREO

A yellow-throated vireo prepares to dine on a luscious bunch of grapes. Limited edition of 50.

This colorful bird has the soft voice of a warbler.

A101. REDPOLL WITH HOLLY & BERRIES COMPOUND

A redpoll sings cheerily in a bough of holly. Limited edition of 50.

This perky little bird has always reminded me of the holiday season.

A102. REDPOLL PANCAKE PLAQUE

On a crisp winter morning, two redpolls gaze proudly from their perch atop a bough of holly on a blue and white ground. One-of-a-kind.

A103. MAGNOLIA WARBLER WITH RASPBERRIES

A magnolia warbler looks hungrily at a ripe raspberry in a thicket.

I designed this weight with the bird amidst one of its favorite foods, raspberries.

A104. RED-BREASTED NUTHATCH

A nuthatch scurries down the trunk of a chestnut tree past a knot hole. Limited edition of 50.

I was always fascinated with how this bird travels headfirst down trees when it is looking for food.

A105. CANADIAN JAY WITH FALL FOLIAGE

A Canadian jay prepares to launch from a beech tree. Limited edition of 50.

An intrepid campsite visitor with a raucous manner. This design is in The Corning Museum of Glass.

A106. PIG & BUNNY

Third in the Glasscape series. A pig and bunny play beneath purple mountains in a grassy meadow. One-of-a-kind.

This weight was commissioned by Frederick Lane to commemorate he and his wife's wedding anniversary. I was honored to create this piece for these childhood sweethearts who are nicknamed "Pig" and "Bunny".

A107. AMERICAN BALD EAGLE HEAD

First in the Wildlife Portrait series. The profile of an eagle captures the magnificence of the species. Limited edition of 50.

I employed the design concepts of antique sulphides to portray the grandeur of the bird, only my portrayal was created entirely with glass.

Detail of A162: Leopard Frog in Marsh with Tiger Lily

A108. CLUSTER OF CLOUDED SULPHUR BUTTERFLIES

First in the Butterfly series. White and yellow clouded sulphur butterflies frolic in a stem of maple leaves on a mauve ground. Limited edition of 50.

My first butterfly and I made it in both color phases. When I was younger I collected these butterflies from a field behind my home.

A109. CLOUDED SULPHUR BUTTERFLIES

Second in the Butterfly series. Two clouded sulphur butterflies flutter over a branch with a pupa (caterpillar) and a chrysalis. Produced on a blue ground with a chrysalis and a white and blue ground without the chrysalis. Limited edition of 50.

A110. CARDINAL IN MEADOWREATHE

A cardinal perches in stems of yellow meadowreathe blossoms in this rare collaboration with Paul Stankard. One-of-a-kind.

A111. BLUE GROSBEAK WITH FOLIAGE

A blue grosbeak lingers in a cluster of frosted elm leaves. Limited edition of 50.

I saw a huge flock of these birds land in an elm tree one day while ice fishing on a lake.

A112. SCARLET MACAW

Eighth in the Tropical Bird series. A scarlet macaw parades its colors on a jungle branch. Limited edition of 75.

This is one of the most spectacularly colored members of the parrot family.

A113. PARULA WARBLER WITH LEAVES & BERRIES

A northern parula warbler roosts atop a leafy branch in a galaxy of blue mulberries. Limited edition of 50.

The smallest warbler in the east and it seems to be a vibrant, happy fellow.

A114. THREE BIRDS IN A TREE

A parula warbler, a mountain bluebird and a chipping sparrow share a patch of brilliant fall foliage. One-of-a-kind.

A115. CHIPPING SPARROW WITH FALL FOLIAGE

A chipping sparrow hops up to a cluster of blue berries in the brilliant changing foliage of an oak tree. Limited edition of 50.

Usually the first bird I heard on my early morning jaunts through the woods before school.

A116. RUBY-CROWN KINGLET WITH RACCOON IN TREE

A ruby-crown kinglet awakens a raccoon burrowed within a tree. Limited edition of 50.

A whimsical approach to a forest encounter.

A117. WESTERN BLUEBIRD

A western bluebird perched in the branches of an ash tree looks into a pale blue sky. Limited edition of 50.

A118. CHIPMUNK & RUBY-CROWN KINGLET

A chipmunk offers a red berry to an eager ruby-crown kinglet on a branch before a blue sky. Limited edition of 25.

This design appealed to my sense of humor and I enjoyed doing it.

A119. YELLOW WARBLER

A yellow warbler is cradled in a branch of hawthorn berries. Limited edition of 50.

Its bobbing tail is often seen in flight across the gardens that surround our home. I find humor in the correlation between this bird's bobbing tail and its song as they seem to happen at the same time.

A120. SNOWY OWL

Fourth in the Bird of Prey series. An elder snowy owl considers his surroundings on a pine branch under a full, yellow moon. One rare piece contains a flying owl. Limited edition of 75.

In my quest for the appropriate scenery to display the awe-inspiring camouflage of this large bird, I discovered the mystifying moon.

A121. WHITE-THROATED SWIFTS IN FLIGHT

A pair of white-throated swifts pursue an insect bathed in the glow of a warm sunset. Limited edition of 50.

These birds are said to be the fastest of all North American birds.

A122. OVENBIRD ON FOREST FLOOR

An ovenbird hops over loose fall foliage past a stem of marigold leaves and red berries. Limited edition of 50.

It took me many hours of searching to come across an ovenbird nest, which are located on the ground and shaped much like a Dutch oven.

A123. HAWAIIAN HONEYCREEPER WITH MISTLETOE BRANCHES

A Hawaiian honeycreeper pouts in branches of white mistletoe berries. Limited edition of 50. Miniature—unlimited.

An endangered bird from the Hawaiian Islands, this colorful bird has a curved bill for getting insects in unusual places.

A124. ROSE-BREASTED GROSBEAK WITH MEADOW FLOWER

A rose-breasted grosbeak perches on the slender stem of a meadow flower, by a bursting seed pod, in this rare collaboration with Paul Stankard. One-of-a-kind.

A125. LOVE BIRDS WITH HEART-SHAPED FACET

Ninth in the Tropical Bird series. Love birds stand on a branch inside a heart-shaped facet. Limited edition of 25.

The heart-shaped facet makes this a rare weight. This design was a surprise Valentine's Day gift for my wife.

A126. BLUE TIT WITH BERRIES

A delicate blue tit stands serenely on a choke cherry branch. Limited edition of 50. Miniature—unlimited.

A perky little European bird.

A127. GOLDEN-BACK ORIOLE WITH NEST & BABIES

A golden-back oriole looks proudly at three peeping chicks in a treetop nest. Limited edition of 50.

A picturesque South American bird.

A128. BLUE-GRAY GNATCATCHER WITH FLOWERS

A blue-gray gnatcatcher warbles in stems of blue forget-me-nots. Limited edition of 50.

This was the first time I created flowers for a paperweight.

A129. CAROLINA WREN WITH IMPATIENS

A Carolina wren eyes a pair of brilliant orange impatiens. Limited edition of 50.

A small secretive bird who runs along the garden floor in order not to be seen.

A130. SUTTON'S WARBLER

A Sutton's warbler takes shelter under a yellow wood sorrel flower. Limited edition of 50. Miniature— unlimited.

This is a hybrid between a parula and a yellow-throated warbler.

A131. SWAINSON'S THRUSH WITH COMMON FLAX

A Swainson's thrush sings longingly in stems of delicate blue common flax flowers. Limited edition of 50. Miniature—unlimited.

This shy bird is found inhabiting moist woods, swamps and thickets.

A132. CARDINAL PROFILE

Second in the Wildlife Portrait series. This lifelike study of a cardinal's head is framed in faceted crystal. Limited edition of 50.

Another example inspired by the design aesthetics of sulphides.

A133. VERMILION FLYCATCHER WITH TRAILING ARBUTUS

A vermilion flycatcher rests on a branch of trailing arbutus flowers over an earth ground. Limited edition of 50. Miniature—unlimited.

Known for its courtship rituals, this picturesque member of the flycatcher family is fairly common and approachable.

A134. MONARCH BUTTERFLY WITH WOOD SORREL

Third in the Butterfly series. A monarch butterfly flutters over a stem of wood sorrel blossoms. Limited edition of 50.

As the world's most common butterfly, the monarch has served as an inspiration for poetry and literature throughout time. I felt compelled to describe its beauty in glass.

A135. RUBY-THROATED HUMMINGBIRD WITH RED TRUMPET FLOWERS

First in the Hummingbird series. A ruby-throated hummingbird drinks sweet nectar from red trumpet flowers. Limited edition of 75. Miniature—unlimited.

The first hummingbird weight. This is the only hummingbird east of the Mississippi River. I was inspired by watching them outside my glass studio, flying in and out of the trumpet flowers.

A136. SCREECH OWL

Fifth in the Bird of Prey series. A screech owl stares into the night from its perch on a pine tree branch with pine cones in this miniature design.

A137. SCREECH OWLS ON PINE BRANCHES

Sixth in the Bird of Prey series. A pair of screech owls rendezvous in the branches of a pine tree. Limited edition of 75.

Known for its mournful song. I decided to portray the two color phases of this bird.

A138. EASTERN BLUEBIRD WITH ASTROMERIA

An eastern bluebird reposes in branches of flowering astromeria blossoms. Limited edition of 75.

Another eastern bluebird design with flowers chosen to enhance the bird's beautiful color.

A139. COTTONTAIL IN SPRING GARDEN

A cottontail bunny frolics in a spring garden with a sulphur butterfly fluttering amidst clover, daisies and dwarf pin cherries. Limited edition of 75.

A design inspired by Peter Rabbit. I'm a romantic that has always had a soft spot for fairy tales.

A140. RED-SHOULDERED HAWK

A red-shouldered hawk eyes the terrain from snow-covered pine branches with pine cones. Limited edition of 75. Miniature—unlimited.

I have always been smitten with these birds of prey, which possess uncanny eyesight and a graceful soar.

A141. CARDINAL IN VIOLETS

A cardinal perches in pink and purple violets in this miniature design. Unlimited.

I always stop to watch this bird when I hike through the fields of upper New Hampshire. It's a very happy experience.

A143. PINK-BREASTED CHAT

A pink-breasted chat clings to a stem of speckled pink dogwood blossoms on an opaque white ground. Limited edition of 50.

A144. CARDINAL WITH CARNATIONS

A bright red cardinal balances on a stem with three pink carnations in this miniature design. Unlimited.

Detail of A145: Eastern Meadowlark with Black-Eyed Susans

A145. EASTERN MEADOWLARK WITH BLACK-EYED SUSANS

A brown and yellow meadowlark twitters a carefree carol to an audience of black-eyed Susans. Limited edition of 75.

A146. HERMIT THRUSH WITH VIOLETS

A hermit thrush scurries under a bouquet of violets and fall leaves. Limited edition of 75.

I was first drawn to this bird because of its awe-inspiring voice. The deep purple of the violets expresses this bird's passionate nature.

A147. YELLOWJACKET NEST WITH APPLE BLOSSOMS

Wasps buzz anxiously around a nest in a blossoming apple tree. Limited edition of 75.

This was my first attempt at wasps. I introduced many techniques that had never been applied to paper-weights before.

A148. WINTER WREN & FLOWERING QUINCE

A winter wren takes a leisurely intermission in a flowering quince tree. Limited edition of 75. Miniature—unlimited.

This is a timid bird with a loud melodious song. It is easily spotted in bare trees during the winter months.

A149. GOLDEN-FRONTED LEAF BIRD WITH GOLDEN SHOWER TREE

Ninth in the Tropical Bird series. A golden-fronted leaf bird muses quietly in a branch of tropical golden shower blossoms. Limited edition of 75.

A South American bird—I was entranced by its color and found some brilliant native flowers to accompany it.

A150. PYRRHOPYGE CREON BUTTERFLY WITH FLOWERS

Fourth in the Butterfly series. A pyrrhopyge creon butterfly spreads imperial blue wings above a blossoming pear tree. Limited edition of 75.

Another excursion into the world of flower pollinators.

A151. PINK-BREASTED LOVE BIRDS

Tenth in the Tropical Bird series. Love birds court in a hammock of pink and blue stylized flowers. Limited edition of 25.

A152. ROBIN WITH FLOWERING DOGWOOD

A robin perches in the center of a triangle of flowering dogwood blossoms. Limited edition of 75. Miniature—unlimited.

Another example of a robin, but this time it is enhanced with flowers.

A153. ROBIN WITH FLOWERING DOGWOOD COMPOUND

A spring robin sings joyously in a flowering dogwood tree. Limited edition of 75.

A154. SCARLET TANAGER WITH TULIP TREE FLOWERS

A scarlet tanager stands on a flowering tulip tree branch. Limited edition of 75. Miniature—unlimited.

A155. SCARLET TANAGER COMPOUND

A scarlet tanager enjoys the fragrance of tulip tree flowers. Limited edition of 75.

I have always enjoyed this bird which clings like a little red jewel to the trees.

A156. WHITE-THROATED MAGPIE JAY WITH RHODODENDRON FLOWERS

A white-throated magpie jay screeches in a stem of pink wild rhododendron flowers. Limited edition of 75. Miniature—unlimited.

I took pleasure in this bird because of its long tail. Jays in particular are striking birds. The rhododendron was chosen to enhance the blue.

A157. WONDERS OF SPRING

A field mouse sits atop a mushroom peering at a sulphur butterfly in a field of crocus blossoms. Limited edition of 50.

With this design I attempted to capture the birth of spring. It was my first mouse weight.

A158. SCARLET-CHESTED PARROT WITH FLAME AMHERSTIA

Eleventh in the Tropical Bird series. A scarlet-chested parrot roosts on a stem of flame amherstia flowers. Limited edition of 75. Miniature—unlimited.

I used a tropical setting to create a vivid display of color.

A159. HEBONIA LEUCIPPE BUTTERFLY WITH DAFFODILS

Fifth in the Butterfly series. A hebonia leucippe butterfly flutters over a stem of daffodils. Limited edition of 75.

The intention was to strive for color harmony and strong realism.

A160. SPRINGTIME IN NEW HAMPSHIRE

A male purple finch, the State Bird of New Hampshire, watches a nest with three blue eggs, in anticipation of the new life to come. The nest is hidden in a field with crocus blossoms, bunch berries and leaves. Limited edition of 35.

This was my first three-dimensional upright bird design—a very big breakthrough. It was also the first time I created a dimensional portrayal of eggs in a nest and my first weight with an earth ground scene. My intent was to examine the ritual of springtime birth.

A161. SPRINGTIME IN NEW HAMPSHIRE WITH FEMALE FINCH

A female purple finch puffs its feathers by a nest with eggs. One-of-a-kind.

A162. LEOPARD FROG IN MARSH WITH LILY PAD

First in series of Pond Life. A leopard frog on a lily pad admires the striking beauty of a floating white lily in a pond with tadpoles. Limited edition of 35.

The first in a series of pond life designs and my first three-dimensional water scene. This weight contained many technical breakthroughs that signaled a turning point in my evolution as an artist. The water with suspended tadpoles advanced the descriptive capabilities of glass art.

A163. BALTIMORE ORIOLE WITH BLACK-EYED SUSANS COMPOUND

A Baltimore oriole cocks its head around to peer at a gathering of black-eyed Susans. Limited edition of 75. Miniature—unlimited.

An attempt to correlate the unique and vivid colors of the black-eyed Susan with the standout oriole.

A164. AMERICAN REDSTART WITH TIGER LILIES

Tiger lilies accent the bright amber markings of an American redstart. Limited edition of 50.

The dimension of these flowers was a technical breakthrough. I was excited by the dramatic color coordination between the orange of the flowers and the black of the bird.

A165. AMERICAN REDSTART WITH TIGER LILIES COMPOUND

An American redstart croons in a spray of tiger lilies. Limited edition of 50.

Tiger lilies are typically enjoyed in floral bouquets. For me they have always been connected with feelings of creativity. The American redstart is among the busiest and brightest of little warblers, and the energy of these two forms compliment each other wonderfully.

A166. SLENDER-SHEARTAIL HUMMINGBIRD WITH FUCHSIA BLOSSOMS

Second in the Hummingbird series. A slender-sheartail hummingbird searches for nectar in a cluster of fuchsia blossoms. Limited edition of 50. Miniature—unlimited.

A comparison of the beautiful delicacy of birds and flowers. This particular design involved a new technique for flowers.

A167. YELLOW-THROATED WARBLER WITH IRIS

A yellow-throated warbler squawks from stems of purple iris flowers. Limited edition of 50.

When I paddle through swampy river areas in my canoe, wild irises are always one of the most recognizable flowers I come across. I felt the warbler's swooping lines coincided nicely with the fine line of the iris.

A168. POINSETTIA BOUQUET

Red and white poinsettias, holly berries, pine needles and pine cones create a festive arrangement. Produced in faceted and unfaceted crystal. Limited edition of 50.

This is my first holiday design. In the spirit of the season, I received a breakthrough on the stamens.

A169. LAMINATED-BILL TOUCAN WITH BIRD OF PARADISE FLOWERS

Twelfth in the Tropical Bird series. A laminated-bill toucan studies its surroundings from stems of blooming bird of paradise flowers. Limited edition of 35.

The dimensional turn of the bird's beak marked a significant advancement in my skills. I chose bird of paradise flowers because they are found in the toucan's natural environment and I was drawn to their intriguing beauty.

Detail of A208: Holiday Bouquet

A170. ROSE-BELLIED BUNTING WITH DOUBLE CHERRY FLOWERS

A rose-bellied bunting balances on delicate stems of pink cherry flowers. Produced on clear or blue ground, in faceted and unfaceted crystal. Limited edition of 35. Miniature—unlimited.

A soft combination of light pinks and blues.

A171. SCARLET TANAGER WITH STRAWBERRY FLOWERS

A flaming scarlet tanager looks for food in a garden of strawberry flowers. Limited edition of 35.

The upright bird designs are the most difficult and challenging pieces I have created in my career.

A172. BROWN THRASHER WITH CHEROKEE ROSES

A brown thrasher trills a sweet melody from a stem of Cherokee roses. Limited edition of 35. Miniature—unlimited.

A173. PAINTED TURTLE WITH VEGETATION

Second in the Pond Life series. A pair of turtles crawl along the lush bank of a pond near a yellow water lily. Snails and vegetation can be seen in the water. Limited edition of 35.

My first turtle weight. I showed great advancement in the turtle and the hidden pond life underwater, including snails and vegetation. This was an extremely challenging design.

A174. PANSY BOUQUET WITH LADYBUGS

A ladybug explores a bouquet with pansies, forget-me-nots, lily buds and clover buds. Produced in faceted and unfaceted crystal. Limited edition of 50.

When I sat in the fields as a youth, the ladybugs crawled around my hands, bringing up feelings of good fortune. Counting the spots was a way of finding lucky numbers. One always hoped to share another moment with a ladybug who bore the same markings.

A175. SALMON-CRESTED COCKATOO WITH CATTLEYA ORCHID

Thirteenth in the Tropical Bird series. A salmon-crested cockatoo poses behind a large cattleya orchid blossom. Produced on clear or blue ground. Limited edition of 50. Miniature—unlimited.

This is my first orchid. I wanted to show this bird in its natural environment.

A176. CHRISTMAS RIBBON BOUQUET

A crimson bow decorates this bouquet containing a poinsettia, pine cones, acorns, holly and Christmas daisies. Limited edition of 50.

This was the first time I attempted to integrate a ribbon into a design.

A177. TITMICE ON SNOWY GROUND

Two titmice commune on stems of snow-covered holly berries with green leaves. Limited edition of 50. Miniature—unlimited.

A winter scene which eventually became a more challenging design when the birds were encased in an upright position. It is always a pleasure to observe these playful birds in the snow.

A178. UPRIGHT TITMICE ON SNOWY GROUND

A pair of titmice hop over a snow bank littered with red and green holly. Limited edition of 50.

A179. GRASSLAND YELLOW FINCH WITH WILD BARBERRY FLOWERS

A dazzling yellow finch poses in a thicket of wild barberry flowers. Limited edition of 50. Miniature—unlimited.

This is the same perky pet many have around the home.

A180. BLACK-CAP CHICKADEE ON HOLLY BRANCH

A black-cap chickadee perches in a stem of holly with red berries in this miniature design. Unlimited.

A181. UPRIGHT BLUE JAY

A blue jay issues a mating call from stems of pink cherry blossoms. One-of-a-kind.

A182. SHEARTAIL HUMMINGBIRD PEDESTAL

A sheartail hummingbird searches for nectar in ruby fuchsia blossoms inside this rare pedestal. One-of-a-kind.

Detail of A265: Walden Pond

1988

A183. PROTHONOTARY WARBLER WITH SPIDERWORT FLOWERS

A prothonotary warbler hides in a group of blue spiderwort flowers. Limited edition of 50. Miniature—unlimited.

This bird prefers to live near swamps or water. In full sunlight its brilliant breast glows like a torch against the dark background of the swamp.

A184. CUPREOUS WITH CINQUEFOILS

Sixth in the Butterfly series. A cupreous butterfly flutters over golden cinquefoils. Limited edition of 50.

A185. BLUEBERRY BOUQUET

Luscious blueberries ripen amidst stems of pink double cherry blossoms. Limited edition of 50. Illusion plaque—limited edition of 50. Miniature—unlimited.

As a child I recall blueberry picking with my sisters and bringing the berries home for my mother's pies and breads. I suppose many people have had similar experiences. I have been told on more than one occasion how much this design stirs up memories. I tried to create a very accurate depiction of the blueberries.

A187. HAWTHORN BERRY BOUQUET

Hawthorn berries hang from stems amidst delicate white blossoms. Limited edition of 50.

The seeds of this plant are spread by various birds and deer, hence hawthorn berries are found throughout fields. I believe on more than one occasion I have carried hawthorns home on socks and pants.

A188. RUBY-CROWN KINGLETS WITH NEST & MORNING GLORIES

A pair of ruby-crown kinglets perch on a nest in a vine of flowering blue morning glories. Limited edition of 50. Miniature—unlimited.

The way the morning glories open and close with dawn and dusk has always amazed me. The kinglet's song is equally fascinating.

A189. BELTED KINGFISHER WITH LADY'S-SLIPPER ORCHIDS & FLOWER GARDEN

A belted kingfisher poses in a cluster of lady's slipper and morning glories. Limited edition of 50.

While fishing along a river bank I have many times watched kingfishers capture the trout I was dreaming about.

A190. SWAMP SPARROW WITH SNOWDROPS & MUSHROOMS

Snowdrops shelter a cheerful swamp sparrow as it eyes a cluster of plump mushrooms. Limited edition of 50.

Due to the shy nature of this bird, I was inclined to include mushrooms in the design. Mushrooms flourish in undisturbed areas—remote shady nooks and moist hiding grounds favored by the sparrow. This was my first dimensional side-view weight.

A191. CHRISTMAS CACTUS BOUQUET

The brilliant red blossoms of a Christmas cactus are arranged with white mistletoe berries and spiky leaves in this festive holiday bouquet. Limited edition of 50.

Another in the series of my holiday season designs. I copied the Christmas cactus from one growing in our home.

A192. TIGER LILY BOUQUET

Dimensional orange tiger lilies and buds create a vibrant design on a lime green ground inside a faceted dome. Limited edition of 50. Miniature—unlimited.

This flower always makes me think of warm summer months.

A193. FALL BOUQUET

An ornate arrangement of Norway spruce, black spruce, white fir and jack pine cones combine with acorns, royal maple leaves, sugar maple leaves, and brick leaves to capture the feeling of the season. Limited edition of 50. Magnum—limited edition of 25.

I tried to capture the splendid display of color during the fall months without using flowers or birds.

A194. AMERICAN PLUM BOUQUET

Luscious ripe plums wait to be plucked from a branch of delicate blossoms. Limited edition of 50. Magnum—limited edition of 10.

One of my first cultivated fruit weights. In order to develop the bloom of the plum, I researched many breakthroughs in color. I wanted to achieve a high level of realism that would make the viewer desire to pick the fruit right off the branch. Anyone who has ever gone fruit picking knows what a special experience this is. I am very proud of the fuzz on the plum.

A195. MAGNOLIA WITH GOLDFINCH

An alert goldfinch enjoys the perfume of an alabaster magnolia blossom. Limited edition of 50.

This three-dimensional bird is uniquely complemented by the large three-dimensional flower.

A196. CHRISTMAS POINSETTIA

This festive holiday bouquet contains a red poinsettia surrounded by white Christmas daisies and red and yellow berries. Limited edition of 50.

I am truly fortunate to have a job that allows me to express the holiday cheer I feel.

A197. SEASCAPE

Fourth in the Glasscape series. A sea gull heads out to sea. Limited edition of 35.

An innovative form of painting with glass on top of a glass disk. It involves quick hands and eyes since the glass cools quickly. This technique combines the skills of traditional painting on canvas with sculpture.

A198. MAGNUM WAVE SCENE

Fifth in the Glasscape series. Sets of turbulent waves pound the shores of a rocky grotto. One-of-a-kind.

A199. LONG-BILLED STAR-THROAT HUMMINGBIRD WITH POLEMONIUMS

Third in the Hummingbird series. A long-billed star-throat hummingbird drinks nectar from a cluster of polemonium blossoms. Limited edition of 50. Miniature—unlimited.

The graceful and lightning quick aesthetics of this hummingbird require little comment. Simply watching fills one with wonder.

A200. RED SALAMANDER IN MARSH

Third in the Pond Life series. A brilliant red salamander crawls toward a white pond lily in a marsh resplendent with quartz rocks, mushrooms and delicate marigolds. Limited edition of 50.

I discovered various shades of salamander underneath the many stones I unearthed in my youth. Nature has equipped this amphibian with a unique ability to change colors. Undoubtedly, red is the most eye-catching tone.

A201. CABBAGE ROSE WITH BUD MAGNUM

A cabbage rose unfolds to reveal numerous pink and mauve petals. One-of-a-kind.

The first rose. The tedious layering of petals has brought me much satisfaction. I chose the cabbage rose because of its size and the subsequent challenge.

A202. CABBAGE ROSE

First in the Rose series. A pink cabbage rose blooms under a sparkling crystal dome. Produced in faceted and unfaceted crystal. Limited edition of 50. Miniature— unlimited.

A203. UPRIGHT ROSE-BELLIED BUNTING WITH DOUBLE CHERRY FLOWERS

A rose-bellied bunting balances on delicate stems of pink cherry flowers. One-of-a-kind.

A soft combination of light pinks and blues.

A204. EUROPEAN BEE-EATER

A European bee-eater prepares to snatch up an unsuspecting bee crawling over an open yellow lily. One-of-a-kind.

1990

A205. CHRYSANTHEMUM BOUQUET

Gold, lavender and rust chrysanthemums twist toward the sun. Limited edition of 25. Miniature—unlimited.

A complicated flower that involved the sealing of many pieces of glass together.

A206. SCISSOR-TAILED FLYCATCHER & BABY

A baby scissor-tailed flycatcher awaits a meal from the mouth of its mother in the branches of a red bud tree with mistletoe. The State Bird, State Flower and State Tree of Oklahoma are featured. Limited edition of 50.

My first three-dimensional baby bird. I was challenged by the flycatcher's long tail.

A207. GREEN FROG ON POND

Fourth in the Pond Life series. A green frog croaks from a lily pad by a floating white pond lily, as content pollywogs wiggle below. Limited of edition of 35.

Another product of my fascination with life in the marsh.

A208. HOLIDAY BOUQUET

Three bright red poinsettias are arranged with red partridge berries and wood anemone flowers in this cheerful holiday design. Limited edition of 50.

A209. APPLE BLOSSOM BOUQUET

Crimson apples ripen on a branch with creamy white blossoms. Limited edition of 50.

The apples captured my curiosity on a crisp fall day in the orchards of a neighboring New Hampshire town.

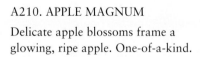

A210. APPLE MAGNUM

Delicate apple blossoms frame a glowing, ripe apple. One-of-a-kind.

A211. EASTERN BLUEBIRD WITH WILD ROSES

Blushing wild roses provide a secluded shelter for a shy eastern bluebird. Limited edition of 50.

A three-dimensional design focused upon the bluebird, who though rarely seen, always instigates feelings of awe and happiness.

A212. FALL BOUQUET PLAQUE

From the Illusion series. Norway spruce, black spruce, white fir, jack pine cones, acorns, royal maple leaves, sugar maple leaves and brick leaves float in a ruby halo. Limited edition of 10.

A213. UPRIGHT FEMALE CARDINAL ON SNOW

A three-dimensional female cardinal hops across a snowy ground in this miniature design. Unlimited.

A214. TITMOUSE ON SNOW

A three-dimensional titmouse eyes a cluster of red holly berries in this miniature design. Unlimited.

A215. CARDINAL IN DOGWOOD

A brilliant red cardinal poses above a white dogwood blossom in this miniature design. Unlimited.

A216. CALIFORNIA QUAIL WITH DESERT SCENE

A California quail pecks around Christmas and barrel cactus in a sandy desert with rocks. Limited edition of 35.

This three-dimensional bird even includes the tuft on its head. The quail is positioned in its natural environment on a realistic desert sand. A great deal of experimenting went into the desert sand. This happens to be one of my favorite weights.

A217. STYLIZED STAR-THROAT HUMMINGBIRD WITH MIRABILIS FLOWERS

Fourth in the Hummingbird series. A stylized star-throat hummingbird searches for nectar in a cluster of mirabilis flowers. Limited edition of 50. Magnum—limited edition of 10. Miniature—unlimited.

Another jewel of the sky. This involved a breakthrough technique on the flower that I have not used since.

A218. POPPY BOUQUET

Brilliant orange poppies bloom amidst wood anemones and blue lilies. Limited edition of 50.

The stamens of the poppy were difficult to design. The red, white and blue blossoms look rich against the green foliage.

A219. OPEN POPPY BOUQUET

A fully opened poppy sits at the center of a bouquet with wood anemones and dimensional blue lilies. One-of-a-kind.

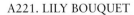

A220. POPPY & PRIMROSE

Vibrant orange poppies, white primrose blossoms and blue flax flowers form a splendid arrangement. One-of-a-kind.

A221. LILY BOUQUET

Wood, Canada and Easter lilies are tied with a bright blue bow to form a colorful bouquet. One-of-a-kind.

A222. SUMMER BOUQUET

A selection of vibrant cosmos blossoms is tied with a pink ribbon. Limited edition of 50.

A223. CARDINAL WITH FLOWERING DOGWOOD

A regal cardinal enjoys a peaceful moment in a flowering dogwood tree.

Official PCA Convention Weight for 1991.

A224. CRAB APPLE BOUQUET

Crisp red and green apples ripen amidst delicate crab apple blossoms. Limited edition of 50.

For many years we have admired our own crab apple trees and the beautiful blooms that fill the front yard each spring.

A225. CRAB APPLE BOUQUET PLAQUE

From the Illusion series. Red and green crab apples float inside a yellow halo. Limited edition of 10.

A226. CHRISTMAS BERRY BOUQUET

Star flowers, marigolds and holly berries form a merry holiday arrangement. Limited edition of 50.

A227. CEDAR WAXWINGS WITH FALL FOLIAGE

Cedar waxwings dine on savory red berries hanging from luminous oak leaves. Limited edition of 50. Miniature—unlimited.

This design was made especially in celebration of our twenty-fifth wedding anniversary. It is my wife's favorite Northern bird.

A228. EXPERIMENTAL YELLOW ROSE WITH BUTTERFLY

A blue butterfly hovers over an open yellow rose. One-of-a-kind.

A229. EXPERIMENTAL YELLOW ROSE WITH LADYBUG

A bright red ladybug crawls towards the velvety yellow petals of a rose. One-of-a-kind.

A230. PINK PEACE

Second in the Rose series. Pink peace roses bloom on stems with blue-green leaves. Limited edition of 50. Magnum—limited edition of 5. Miniature—unlimited.

My first garden rose. It was a simple, pretty and refreshing breakthrough in realism and dimension.

A231. PINK PEACE PLAQUE

From the Illusion series. Pink peace roses bloom inside a cobalt blue halo. Limited edition of 10.

A232. FAMILY OF DUCKS ON A POND

Fifth in the Pond Life series. A family of mallard ducks paddles toward the mossy shore of a tranquil green pond. Limited edition of 50.

A realistic approach influenced by the antique weight Ducks on the Pond. *I felt capable of bringing the design much further than the original. I have many fond memories of watching my children feed crackers to mallards.*

A233. WHITE POND LILY WITH DRAGONFLY

An iridescent blue dragonfly hovers over a glorious white pond lily. One-of-a-kind.

A234. SWAMP SPARROW

From the Illusion series. A swamp sparrow perches by mushrooms near a group of white snowdrop flowers inside a white halo. Limited edition of 10.

Detail of A232: Family of Ducks on a Pond

A235. CAT WITH BLUEBIRD

A cat meows at a friendly bluebird perched amidst spring tulips and crocus blossoms. Limited edition of 5.

A236. SPLENDID COPPER BUTTERFLY

Seventh in the Butterfly series. A splendid copper butterfly flutters over a bed of golden funnel flowers. Limited edition of 50.

A237. YELLOW-BREASTED CHATS

A yellow-breasted chat serenades its partner as eggs nestle peacefully below. Limited edition of 50.

An extremely intricate three-dimensional side view. Creating this weight with the beak open was an important advancement for later works. The delicate nest was constructed piece by piece out of glass twigs I created. These birds are known for singing to the moon on luminous nights.

A238. AMERICAN BALD EAGLE

First in the Endangered Species series. An American bald eagle perches on the top of a pine tree amidst pine cones. Limited edition of 50.

A large three-dimensional bird which is difficult to create because of its size. When I began the Endangered Species series there was little question about whether or not I would create an eagle. The tradition and strength that surround this bird have always filled me with respect and admiration.

A239. LE BOUQUET DE PRINTEMPS

Radiant daffodil blossoms mingle with white snow berries and buds. Limited edition of 50.

I wanted to express my springtime joy with these vibrant yellow flowers.

A240. BLACK CHERRY BOUQUET

A cherry tree branch bursts with white blossoms and cherries in different stages of ripeness. Limited edition of 50.

Depicting the cherries in different stages of ripeness made this design difficult to create. Cherries play an important part in Japanese folklore.

A241. PARADISEA

Eighth in the Butterfly series. A paradisea butterfly flutters above soft-hued cosmos blossoms. Limited edition of 50.

The intricate color combinations of this butterfly sparked my interest. My technical ability was challenged by the wings.

A242. AMERICAN BEAUTY RED ROSE BOUQUET

Third in the Rose series. American beauty red roses mingle with delicate baby's breath in this elegant bouquet. Limited edition of 50. Miniature—unlimited.

The red rose symbolizes first love, and I have admired its velvety petals for many years.

Detail of A257: American Beauty Red Rose Bouquet Magnum

A243. TIGER LILY BOUQUET WITH COSMOS

The stunning beauty of a tiger lily is accented with cosmos blossoms. One-of-a-kind.

A244. ABOVE THE CANOPY

Fourteenth in the Tropical Bird series. A yellow-headed Amazon parrot roosts on a limb of red tropical paradise flowers. Limited edition of 50. Miniature—unlimited.

I chose this parrot for its array of colors.

A245. AMAZON PARROTS MAGNUM PLAQUE

Fifteenth in the Tropical Bird series. Two yellow-headed Amazon parrots socialize in branches of tropical paradise flowers in this upright design, which is set on an emerald ground. Limited edition of 10.

I chose the translucent green background to further emphasize the feeling of jungle.

A246. SPRING

First in the Four Seasons Bouquet series. A bouquet of crocus, iris, forget-me-nots, wax flowers, violets and narcissus blossoms cheerfully announce the arrival of spring. Limited edition of 50.

I made this weight to lift the spirits of all those who were down trodden by the lifeless winter.

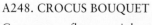

A247. SPRING BOUQUET

From the Illusion series. Forget-me-nots, wax flowers, violets and narcissus bloom in a cobalt blue halo. Limited edition of 10.

A248. CROCUS BOUQUET

Crocus, wax flowers, violets and narcissus flowers create a bright tapestry of color. Limited edition of 50.

A249. WIND RUSH

Red and white Japanese anemones bloom on a black ground. Limited edition of 50.

The dramatic red and white flowers against the black background enhance the elegance of this bouquet.

A251. SOUTHERN PEACH

Mockingbirds croon merrily to an audience of peach blossoms. Limited edition of 50. Miniature—unlimited.

A sweet portrait of a common Southern sight. These three-dimensional birds not only have an open beak, but also a red tongue.

A252. BREATH OF LIFE

Fourth in the Rose series. Delicate yellow roses unfurl on green stems in this elegant bouquet. Limited edition of 50. Miniature—unlimited.

The vibrant yellow excites me. Plus, this rose is my wife's favorite flower.

A253. NOCTURNAL COURTSHIP

First in the Spirit of the Tropical Rain Forest series. Red-eyed tree frogs cling to stems of flaming sword flowers. Limited edition of 50.

My idea was to create two frogs meeting in the treetops at night. The rain forest is miles deep with priceless creatures which compel me to create honorific monuments to their beauty.

A254. WINTER TRUCE

A pair of red cardinals perch in branches of snow-covered holly leaves and winter berries. Limited edition of 50. Miniature—unlimited.

I was striving to create a strong sense of winter. Cardinals are very territorial birds and one wouldn't ordinarily find two males in a branch like one sees here, thus the name of the piece, Winter Truce.

A255. MIDNIGHT VIGIL

Second in the Endangered Species series. A spotted owl watches over its fledgling beneath a full, yellow moon. Limited edition of 50. Miniature—unlimited.

I created a pitch-black nighttime atmosphere for this large, deeply speculative bird.

A256. FUCHSIA FROLIC

Fifth in the Hummingbird series. A pair of purple-throated sapphire hummingbirds drink the nectar from a cluster of fuchsia blossoms. Limited edition of 50. Miniature—unlimited.

The purple bird used in combination with the fuchsia created a nice mood within this design.

A257. AMERICAN BEAUTY RED ROSE BOUQUET MAGNUM

American beauty red roses promise a velvet touch and rich fragrance. Limited edition of 5.

A258. LE BOUQUET DE PRINTEMPS PLAQUE

From the Illusion series. Bright yellow daffodils bloom inside a royal blue halo. Limited edition of 10.

A259. AMERICAN BEAUTY PLAQUE

From the Illusion series. American beauty roses bloom within a ruby halo. Limited edition of 10.

A260. AMERICAN BEAUTY SPIRAL

From the Illusion series. American beauty red roses bloom inside a cobalt blue halo, in an upright plaque with spiral cutting. Limited edition of 10.

A261. NEW LIFE

A pair of newborn house wrens chirp hungrily from a nest in the branches of a magnolia tree, as their guardians deliver the morning meal. Limited edition of 50.

My first three-dimensional babies in a nest weight. I consider this to be one of the best examples of lamp-work I ever created. This design mimics a moment in nature that I have had the pleasure of observing.

A262. ENGLISH GARDEN

Tiger lilies, delphiniums, and marigolds congregate to produce a splendid display. Limited edition of 50.

While walking through a friend's flower garden I was struck with this design. While it may not really exist, it is how I envision an English garden.

A263. SWEET SUMMER

Second in the Four Seasons Bouquet series. Carnations, daisies, mini mums and freesias combine to form a delightful portrait of summer. Limited edition of 50.

I enjoyed the light summer feeling of this arrangement.

A264. SWEET SUMMER PLAQUE

From the Illusion series. Carnations, daisies, mini mums and freesias bloom in a vibrant fuchsia halo. Limited edition of 10.

A265. WALDEN POND

Sixth in the Pond Life series. A pond slider turtle peeks from the depths of a shimmering pond at another turtle crawling across a mossy bank overgrown with wild arum flowers in this magnum design. Produced with a blue or green pond. Limited edition of 25. Miniature—unlimited.

After researching the shell of the turtle for over two months, I finally reached an advancement in realism and form. The new technique involved in presenting the turtle that lies below the pond's surface has opened up a new ability to capture an entire picture of the habitat surrounding and affecting the turtle. The pond was created with both a blue and a more realistic green water. It has brought me great pleasure to be able to support the Walden Woods Foundation with profits from this piece, since their philosophy supports not only the arts, but also the environment.

A266. FUCHSIA FROLIC PLAQUE

From the Illusion series. Purple-throated sapphire hummingbirds drink the nectar from a cluster of fuchsia blossoms inside an amethyst halo. Limited edition of 10.

A267. SPRING BOUQUET RAINBOW

From the Illusion series. Forget-me-nots, wax flowers, violets and narcissus bloom in a multicolored halo containing all the colors of the rainbow. Limited edition of 10.

A268. AMERICAN BEAUTY EGG

Large three-dimensional roses bloom in a faceted egg that multiplies the imagery. One-of-a-kind.

A269. A TOUCH OF CLASS ROSEBUSH TRIPLE

A touch of class pink roses bloom in this three-tiered crystal presentation piece. Limited edition of 5.

A270. AMERICAN BEAUTY ROSEBUSH TRIPLE

American beauty red roses bloom with delicate white wildflowers and buds in this impressive display. Limited edition of 5.

A271. BREATH OF LIFE PLAQUE

From the Illusion series. An arrangement of breath of life roses and white daisy buds floats in a turquoise halo. Limited edition of 10.

A272. BREATH OF LIFE ROSEBUSH TRIPLE

Yellow breath of life roses bloom amidst white daisy buds in this three-tiered display. Limited edition of 5.

A273. THE QUINTESSENTIAL ROSEBUSH TRIPLE

Pink peace, a touch of class and American beauty red roses bloom in this elegant triple-tiered presentation piece. Limited edition of 5.

A274. THE CONSUMMATE ROSEBUSH TRIPLE

Pink peace, breath of life and American beauty red roses unfurl in a triple-tiered crystal masterpiece. Limited edition of 5.

A275. THE FABULOUS ROSE WEIGHT

Pink peace, a touch of class and American
beauty roses bloom on a single stem in
this triumphant creation. One-of-a-kind.

A276. A TOUCH OF CLASS

Fifth in the Rose series. A touch-of-class roses unfold to reveal vibrant mauve and pink petals. Limited edition of 50. Miniature—unlimited.

I was attempting to replicate the roses outside of my studio.

A277. BLACK ROSE

A velvety black rose blooms in a crystal dome in this miniature design. One-of-a-kind.

A278. PARADISE

Sixth in the Hummingbird series. A beautiful hummingbird flitters around a bunch of paradise lilies. Limited edition of 50. Miniature—unlimited.

I strove for a colorful design capable of gaining the attention of any eye. The numerous colors of this glittering hummingbird species contrasts wonderfully with the stem of lilies.

A279. ENCHANTMENT

Pink and white lady's-slipper orchids, carnations and pink mink protea cast an enchanting spell. Limited edition of 50.

Lady's slippers are rare orchids and I am fortunate to have several in the woods behind our home. They inspired this soft pink theme.

A280. SYMPHONY

Pink, mauve and purple peonies bloom amidst a sea of tiny wildflowers on stems with violet-tinged caladium leaves. Each magnificent peony blossom is formed from more than fifty delicate petals. Limited edition of 50. Miniature—unlimited.

A beautiful flower, simply displayed.

A281. TURTLE & DRAGONFLY

An iridescent blue dragonfly hovers over a pond slider turtle crawling through dried grass with pale blue forget-me-nots and pink wild roses, in this special collaboration with Paul Stankard. Limited edition of 5.

A282. ON GOLDEN POND

Seventh in the Pond Life series. A loon paddles gracefully past floating yellow water lilies in this scene, named after one of the artist's favorite ice fishing spots. A rainbow trout attempts to elude a second diving loon. A mossy bank with blueberries, white daisies and pink hepatica rests at the pond's edge in this magnum design. Limited edition of 25.

This design brought breakthroughs in the feathering technique of the bird and in many areas of lampwork. It was a pleasure to be able to reproduce one of the most enjoyable sights that I have shared with my family in the upper lakes of New Hampshire. The loon is a truly remarkable bird, capable of arousing deep emotion through its desperate, soulful song.

A283. MISTY MORNINGS

Third in the Four Seasons Bouquet series. Delicate wildflowers and brilliant marigolds combine to form this stunning fall bouquet. Limited edition of 50.

The numerous individual petals of the marigold bring a delightful dimensionality and realism to this bouquet.

A284. ANGELICA

From the Illusion series. A pair of cherubs share a kiss above a peony bouquet inside a pink halo. Limited edition of 5.

The faces of the cherubs, measuring less than an eighth of an inch, were a true test of my skill.

A285. PARADISE PLAQUE

From the Illusion series. A beautiful hummingbird hovers by paradise lilies inside a golden yellow halo in this masterful upright display. Limited edition of 5.

A286. IN THE TREETOP

From the Emergence series. A cardinal nests at the top of a flowering dogwood tree in this special collaboration with Steven Lundberg. The lampwork cardinal is placed outside the dome of the paperweight. Limited edition of 5.

A287. BALLERINA

Sixth in the Rose series. Three delicate pink ballerina roses unfurl on vibrant green stems. Limited edition of 50. Miniature—unlimited.

A288. BALLERINA POND MAGNUM

A large pink ballerina rose floats in a turquoise pond. Limited edition of 10.

A289. BALLERINA SPIRAL

From the Illusion series. Delicate pink roses float inside a jewellike blue halo in a crystal plaque with spiral cutting. Limited edition of 5.

A290. SPRINGTIME IN MALLORCA

A European robin sings in the branches of a blossoming almond tree. Limited edition of 50. Miniature— unlimited.

A291. PASSING GLORY

Ninth in the Butterfly series. A pink *rhodophthitus simplex roseus* butterfly flutters over lavender clematis blossoms. Limited edition of 50.

This is the only pink butterfly to exist in nature.

A292. BLUEBERRY HILL

A mountain bluebird holds a worm in its beak above a nest with three peeping fledglings in the branches of a loaded blueberry bush. Limited edition of 25.

This was my first three-dimensional design to feature open-mouthed birds in a nest. Each fledgling measures one-quarter inch in height.

A293. BLACK-THROATED BLUE WARBLER WITH WILD COLUMBINES

First in the Audubon series. Ayotte recreates the magic of naturalist John James Audubon's prints in this design, inspired by plate 349 from the *Elephant Folio*. Limited edition of 50.

This was my first attempt at reproducing an Audubon print. The work of this naturalist is an obvious inspiration. I have spent countless hours studying his prints.

A294. WHITE MOUNTAIN BOUQUET

Red and white lilies grow on stems with vibrant red, white and blue buds, pale blue and white leaves, and green tendrils. Limited edition of 35.

A295. DRINK OF LIFE

Seventh in the Hummingbird series. A pair of rose-throated flame bearer hummingbirds drink nectar from red trumpet honeysuckle blossoms. Limited edition of 50.

A technical breakthrough enabled me to show the hummingbirds actually drinking from the flower.

A296. ANTICIPATION

First in the Nature's Camouflage series. A goldenrod spider waits for a housefly on a marsh marigold. Limited edition of 25.

A297. MIDNIGHT BLUE

From the Glasscape series. Frothing ocean waves surge through the mouth of a cave in this panoramic glass painting. In some pieces a sea gull flies through the sky.

I consider this to be my best work to date. The numerous "painted" layers of glass instill the design with a superb authenticity. This new technique opens the door for more fascinating paintings in this area.

A298. BERGUNDER CHRYSANTHEMUM

This extremely dimensional rust-colored flower with upright yellow stamens blooms in a crystal miniature. Unlimited.

A299. STARGAZER LILY

A white-edged pink and white lily serves as a beautiful visual poem in this precious miniature. Unlimited.

A300. MOTHER NATURE

A baby chipmunk hides from its mother in the hollow of a log as she scurries across a forest floor towards an acorn. The realistic three-dimensional scene includes brilliant fall leaves, a pine cone, mushrooms, white daisies, wild arum flowers and blue forget-me-nots. Limited edition of 25.

A301. MISTY BLUE

Seventh in the Rose series. This large life-sized pink and periwinkle annual blooms on a thorny stem with deep maroon leaves. Limited edition of 25. Miniature—unlimited.

A302. CARIBBEAN NIGHT

A sea tortoise surges through a jewellike Caribbean sea. Limited edition of 25.

Sea turtles usually come out at night. I wanted to celebrate this rare nighttime sight.

A303. PANSY

A velvety pansy is portrayed in shades of pink, purple or blue in this miniature design. Unlimited.

A304. POINSETTIA

A brilliant red poinsettia with yellow stamens blooms in this miniature design. Unlimited.

A305. ROSE BUD

From the Denali Collaborations series. Rick Ayotte crafted a delicate opening red rosebud for this dimensional presentation. This collaboration with the artists from Denali Crystal is encased in a flame-cut optical crystal exterior enhanced with a ruby-dye that emphasizes the themes of passion and romance that surround the flower.

A306. LADY'S-SLIPPER RADIANCE

From the Denali Collaborations series. Carnations, pink mink protea and lady's-slipper orchids bloom in this symmetrical diamond-cut sculpture created in collaboration with Denali Crystal. The carefully laminated design creates a spectacular halo of radiance around the flowers.

A307. HONEYSUCKLE RADIANCE

From the Denali Collaborations series. A rose-throated flame bearer hummingbird searches for nectar in a cluster of honeysuckle blossoms in this innovative design. The imagery is set in an optical crystal spire with symmetrical radiating lines expanding towards the viewer to create a dimension of vibrant elastic space in the piece. A backdrop composed of colorful floral reflections helps enhance the feeling that the hummingbird is searching for nectar in a larger plant.

A308. FLOWER BUD

From the Denali Collaborations series. A pink and white lady's-slipper orchid is presented in a flame-cut optical crystal exterior that bends the imagery into abstract stripes of color at the edges of the piece.

Miniatures: Simplified Beauty

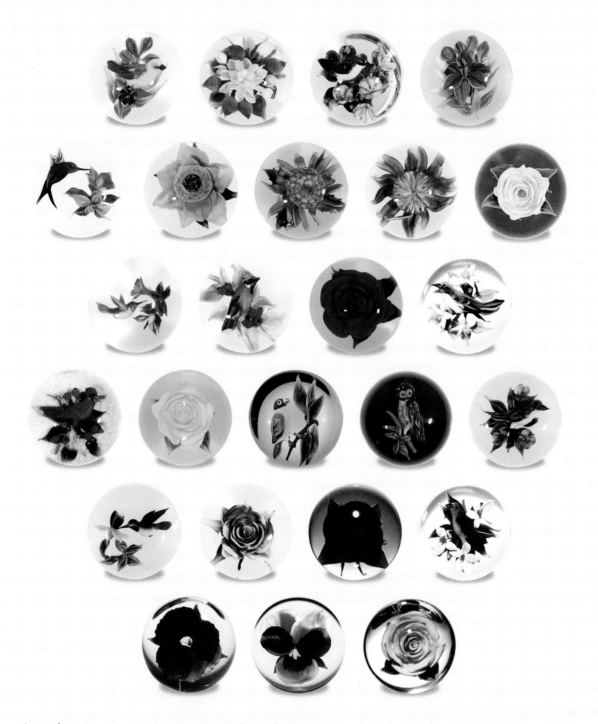

Ayotte began creating miniature paperweights with the intention of making his glasswork affordable to all who enjoyed it, however, this aspect of his glassworking quickly took on a life and direction of its own. Many of these designs, such as the velvety black rose and the stargazer lily, incorporate imagery unique to the miniature format. One also finds a number of rare artist proof miniatures. These study pieces were created in the process of mapping out a larger design. Ayotte's miniature animated worlds have delighted countless collectors across the globe.

Collectors' Checklist

1978

❏ A1. Male Cardinal

❏ A2. Male Wood Thrush

1979

❏ A3. Male & Female Cardinal

❏ A4. Open-Wing Wood Thrush

❏ A5. Male Goldfinch

❏ A6. Male & Female Goldfinch

❏ A7. Female Goldfinch

❏ A8. Scarlet Tanager

❏ A9. Male Scarlet Tanager

❏ A10. Male & Female Scarlet Tanager

❏ A11. Scarlet Tanager in Flight

❏ A12. Goldfinch & Scarlet Tanager

❏ A13. Female Scarlet Tanager

❏ A14. Eastern Bluebirds

❏ A15. Singing Bluebird Compound

❏ A16. Eastern Bluebird in Flight

❏ A17. Robin on Branch

❏ A18. Mother Robin with Baby

❏ A19. Downy Woodpecker

❏ A20. Woodpecker in Flight

❏ A21. Male Towhee

❏ A22. Black-Cap Chickadee

❏ A23. Female Cardinal

❏ A24. Male Cardinal in Flight

❏ A25. California Quail

❏ A26. Yellow-Throated Warbler

❏ A27. Yellow-Throated Warblers in Reeds

❏ A28. Baltimore Oriole

❏ A29. Male Baltimore Oriole with Nest

❏ A30. Sparrow Hawk

1980

❏ A31. Eastern Bluebirds Compound

❏ A32. Purple Finch on Snow

❏ A33. Peregrine Falcon on Blue

❏ A34. Blackburnian Warbler on Pine Needles

❏ A35. Blue & Gold Macaw—
First in the Tropical Bird series

❏ A36. Male & Female Macaw Parrots—
Second in the Tropical Bird series

❏ A37. Redheaded Woodpecker

❏ A38. Woodpeckers with Clouds Compound

❏ A39. Downy Woodpecker with Raccoon

❏ A40. Hawk Owl—
First in the Bird of Prey series

❏ A41. Hawk Owl with Moon—
Second in the Bird of Prey series

❏ A42. Hawk Owl Double Compound—
Third in the Bird of Prey series

❏ A43. Herring Sea Gull

❏ A44. Herring Sea Gull in Flight

❏ A45. Herring Sea Gull & Sandpiper

❏ A46. Herring Sea Gulls Compound

❏ A47. Redheaded Woodpecker

❏ A48. Redheaded Woodpeckers

❏ A49. Mallard Duck with Cattails

❏ A50. Mallard Duck Female

❏ A51. Mallard Duck on a Pond Compound

❏ A52. Mallard Duck in Flight

❏ A53. Western Meadowlark

❏ A54. Western Meadowlark with Rainbow

❏ A55. Crissel Thrasher

❏ A56. Great White Heron on a Log

❏ A57. Great White Heron Compound

❏ A58. Great White Heron & Frog

❏ A59. House Wren

❏ A60. House Wren with Sun

❏ A61. Male & Female House Wren

❏ A62. Bluebird & Goldfinch

❏ A63. Marsh Wren with Nest

❏ A64. Sulphur-Crested Cockatoo—
Third in the Tropical Bird series

❏ A65. Sulphur-Crested Cockatoos Compound—
Fourth in the Tropical Bird series

❏ A66. Baltimore Oriole with Acorns Compound

1981

- ❑ A67. Rose-Breasted Grosbeak
- ❑ A68. Rose-Breasted Grosbeak with Fledglings
- ❑ A69. Rose-Breasted Grosbeak Female
- ❑ A70. Rose-Breasted Grosbeak Male
- ❑ A71. Mute Swan
- ❑ A72. Yellow-Billed Cuckoo
- ❑ A73. Yellow-Billed Cuckoos
- ❑ A74. Wood Thrush with Oak Leaves
- ❑ A75. Male & Female Wood Thrush
- ❑ A76. Keel-Billed Toucan—
  Fifth in the Tropical Bird series
- ❑ A77. Keel-Billed Toucan Compound—
  Sixth in the Tropical Bird series
- ❑ A78. The Great Flamingo with Palm Tree
  Compound—*Seventh in the Tropical Bird series*
- ❑ A79. Painted Bunting
- ❑ A80. Robin with Three Chicks
- ❑ A81. Ocean Scene—*First in the Glasscape series*
- ❑ A82. Brown Thrasher in Poison Sumac Leaves
- ❑ A83. Eastern Phoebe with Grapes & Foliage
- ❑ A84. Chestnut-Sided Warbler
- ❑ A85. Dickcissel with Pine Cones
- ❑ A86. Barn Swallow with Bug
- ❑ A87. Barn Swallow
- ❑ A88. White-Crown Sparrow
- ❑ A89. Western Tanager
- ❑ A90. Western Tanager in Fall Foliage
- ❑ A91. Carolina Chickadee
- ❑ A92. Dancing Unicorns

1982

- ❑ A93. Blue Jay
- ❑ A94. Blue Jay Near Stream—
  Second in the Glasscape series
- ❑ A95. House Sparrows
- ❑ A96. White-Crown Sparrow with Rose
- ❑ A97. Sparrow
- ❑ A98. Black-Cap Chickadee
  with Wood Sorrel Cube
- ❑ A99. Chickadee with Pine Cones Compound
- ❑ A100. Yellow-Throated Vireo
- ❑ A101. Redpoll with Holly & Berries Compound
- ❑ A102. Redpoll Pancake Plaque

- ❑ A103. Magnolia Warbler with Raspberries
- ❑ A104. Red-Breasted Nuthatch
- ❑ A105. Canadian Jay with Fall Foliage
- ❑ A106. Pig & Bunny—
  Third in the Glasscape series
- ❑ A107. American Bald Eagle Head—
  First in the Wildlife Portrait series

1983

- ❑ A108. Cluster of Clouded Sulphur Butterflies—
  First in the Butterfly series
- ❑ A109. Clouded Sulphur Butterflies—
  Second in the Butterfly series
- ❑ A110. Cardinal in Meadowreathe
- ❑ A111. Blue Grosbeak with Foliage
- ❑ A112. Scarlet Macaw—
  Eighth in the Tropical Bird series
- ❑ A113. Parula Warbler with Leaves & Berries
- ❑ A114. Three Birds in a Tree
- ❑ A115. Chipping Sparrow with Fall Foliage
- ❑ A116. Ruby-Crown Kinglet with Raccoon in Tree
- ❑ A117. Western Bluebird
- ❑ A118. Chipmunk & Ruby-Crown Kinglet
- ❑ A119. Yellow Warbler
- ❑ A120. Snowy Owl—
  Fourth in the Bird of Prey series
- ❑ A121. White-Throated Swifts in Flight
- ❑ A122. Ovenbird on Forest Floor
- ❑ A123. Hawaiian Honeycreeper
  with Mistletoe Branches
- ❑ A124. Rose-Breasted Grosbeak
  with Meadow Flower

1984

- ❑ A125. Love Birds with Heart-Shaped Facet—
  Ninth in the Tropical Bird series
- ❑ A126. Blue Tit with Berries
- ❑ A127. Golden-Back Oriole with Nest & Babies
- ❑ A128. Blue-Gray Gnatcatcher with Flowers
- ❑ A129. Carolina Wren with Impatiens
- ❑ A130. Sutton's Warbler
- ❑ A131. Swainson's Thrush with Common Flax
- ❑ A132. Cardinal Profile—
  Second in the Wildlife Portrait series
- ❑ A133. Vermilion Flycatcher
  with Trailing Arbutus

- A134. Monarch Butterfly with Wood Sorrel—
  Third in the Butterfly series
- A135. Ruby-Throated Hummingbird
  with Red Trumpet Flowers—
  First in the Hummingbird series
- A136. Screech Owl—
  Fifth in the Bird of Prey series
- A137. Screech Owls on Pine Branches—
  Sixth in the Bird of Prey series
- A138. Eastern Bluebird with Astromeria
- A139. Cottontail in Spring Garden
- A140. Red-Shouldered Hawk
- A141. Cardinal in Violets
- A142. Mockingbird with Magnolia
- A143. Pink-Breasted Chat
- A144. Cardinal with Carnations

1985

- A145. Eastern Meadowlark
  with Black-Eyed Susans
- A146. Hermit Thrush with Violets
- A147. Yellowjacket Nest with Apple Blossoms
- A148. Winter Wren & Flowering Quince
- A149. Golden-Fronted Leaf Bird with Golden
  Shower Tree—*Ninth in the Tropical Bird series*
- A150. Pyrrhopyge Creon Butterfly with Flowers—
  Fourth in the Butterfly series
- A151. Pink-Breasted Love Birds—
  Tenth in the Tropical Bird series
- A152. Robin with Flowering Dogwood
- A153. Robin with Flowering Dogwood
  Compound
- A154. Scarlet Tanager with Tulip Tree Flowers
- A155. Scarlet Tanager Compound

1986

- A156. White-Throated Magpie Jay
  with Rhododendron Flowers
- A157. Wonders of Spring
- A158. Scarlet-Chested Parrot with Flame
  Amherstia—*Eleventh in the Tropical Bird series*
- A159. Hebonia Leucippe Butterfly with
  Daffodils—*Fifth in the Butterfly series*
- A160. Springtime in New Hampshire
- A161. Springtime in New Hampshire
  with Female Finch
- A162. Leopard Frog in Marsh with Lily Pad—
  First in the Pond Life Series

- A163. Baltimore Oriole
  with Black-Eyed Susans Compound
- A164. American Redstart with Tiger Lilies
- A165. American Redstart with Tiger Lilies
  Compound
- A166. Slender-Sheartail Hummingbird
  with Fuchsia Blossoms—
  Second in the Hummingbird series
- A167. Yellow-Throated Warbler with Iris
- A168. Poinsettia Bouquet
- A169. Laminated-Bill Toucan
  with Bird of Paradise—
  Twelfth in the Tropical Bird series

1987

- A170. Rose-Bellied Bunting
  with Double Cherry Flowers
- A171. Scarlet Tanager with Strawberry Flowers
- A172. Brown Thrasher with Cherokee Roses
- A173. Painted Turtle with Vegetation—
  Second in the Pond Life series
- A174. Pansy Bouquet with Ladybugs
- A175. Salmon-Crested Cockatoo with Cattleya
  Orchid—*Thirteenth in the Tropical Bird series*
- A176. Christmas Ribbon Bouquet
- A177. Titmice on Snowy Ground
- A178. Upright Titmice on Snowy Ground
- A179. Grassland Yellow Finch
  with Wild Barberry Flowers
- A180. Black-Cap Chickadee on Holly Branch
- A181. Upright Blue Jay
- A182. Sheartail Hummingbird Pedestal

1988

- A183. Prothonotary Warbler
  with Spiderwort Flowers
- A184. Cupreous with Cinquefoils—
  Sixth in the Butterfly series
- A185. Blueberry Bouquet
- A186. Southern Magnolia with Mockingbird
- A187. Hawthorn Berry Bouquet
- A188. Ruby-Crown Kinglets with Nest
  & Morning Glories
- A189. Belted Kingfisher with Lady's-Slippers
  Orchids & Flower Garden
- A190. Swamp Sparrow
  with Snowdrops & Mushrooms

- ❏ A191. Christmas Cactus Bouquet
- ❏ A192. Tiger Lily Bouquet
- ❏ A193. Fall Bouquet

1989

- ❏ A194. American Plum Bouquet
- ❏ A195. Magnolia with Goldfinch
- ❏ A196. Christmas Poinsettia
- ❏ A197. Seascape—*Fourth in the Glasscape series*
- ❏ A198. Magnum Wave Scene— *Fifth in the Glasscape series*
- ❏ A199. Long-Billed Star-Throat Hummingbird with Polemoniums— *Third in the Hummingbird series*
- ❏ A200. Red Salamander in Marsh— *Third in the Pond Life series*
- ❏ A201. Cabbage Rose with Bud Magnum
- ❏ A202. Cabbage Rose—*First in the Rose series*
- ❏ A203. Upright Rose-Bellied Bunting with Double Cherry Flowers
- ❏ A204. European Bee-Eater

1990

- ❏ A205. Chrysanthemum Bouquet
- ❏ A206. Scissor-Tailed Flycatcher & Baby
- ❏ A207. Green Frog on Pond— *Fourth in the Pond Life series*
- ❏ A208. Holiday Bouquet
- ❏ A209. Apple Blossom Bouquet
- ❏ A210. Apple Magnum
- ❏ A211. Eastern Bluebird with Wild Roses
- ❏ A212. Fall Bouquet Plaque *from the Illusion series*
- ❏ A213. Upright Female Cardinal on Snow
- ❏ A214. Titmouse on Snow
- ❏ A215. Cardinal in Dogwood

1991

- ❏ A216. California Quail with Desert Scene
- ❏ A217. Stylized Star-Throat Hummingbird with Mirabilis Flowers— *Fourth in the Hummingbird series*
- ❏ A218. Poppy Bouquet
- ❏ A219. Open Poppy Bouquet
- ❏ A220. Poppy & Primrose
- ❏ A221. Lily Bouquet
- ❏ A222. Summer Bouquet

- ❏ A223. Cardinal with Flowering Dogwood
- ❏ A224. Crab Apple Bouquet
- ❏ A225. Crab Apple Bouquet Plaque *from the Illusion series*
- ❏ A226. Christmas Berry Bouquet
- ❏ A227. Cedar Waxwings with Fall Foliage
- ❏ A228. Experimental Yellow Rose with Butterfly
- ❏ A229. Experimental Yellow Rose with Ladybug
- ❏ A230. Pink Peace—*Second in the Rose series*
- ❏ A231. Pink Peace Plaque *from the Illusion series*
- ❏ A232. Family of Ducks on a Pond— *Fifth in the Pond Life series*
- ❏ A233. White Pond Lily with Dragonfly
- ❏ A234. Swamp Sparrow *from the Illusion series*

1992

- ❏ A235. Cat with Bluebird
- ❏ A236. Splendid Copper Butterfly— *Seventh in the Butterfly series*
- ❏ A237. Yellow-Breasted Chats
- ❏ A238. American Bald Eagle— *First in the Endangered Species series*
- ❏ A239. Le Bouquet de Printemps
- ❏ A240. Black Cherry Bouquet
- ❏ A241. Paradisea—*Eighth in the Butterfly series*
- ❏ A242. American Beauty Red Rose Bouquet— *Third in the Rose series*

1993

- ❏ A243. Tiger Lily Bouquet with Cosmos
- ❏ A244. Above the Canopy— *Fourteenth in the Tropical Bird series*
- ❏ A245. Amazon Parrots Magnum Plaque— *Fifteenth in the Tropical Bird series*
- ❏ A246. Spring—*First in the Four Seasons Bouquet series*
- ❏ A247. Spring Bouquet *from the Illusion series*
- ❏ A248. Crocus Bouquet
- ❏ A249. Wind Rush
- ❏ A250. Mockingbird with Orange Blossoms
- ❏ A251. Southern Peach
- ❏ A252. Breath of Life—*Fourth in the Rose series*
- ❏ A253. Nocturnal Courtship—*First in the Spirit of the Tropical Rain Forest series*
- ❏ A254. Winter Truce
- ❏ A255. Midnight Vigil— *Second in the Endangered Species series*

- ❏ A256. Fuchsia Frolic—
  Fifth in the Hummingbird series
- ❏ A257. American Beauty Red Rose Bouquet Magnum
- ❏ A258. Le Bouquet de Printemps Plaque
  from the Illusion series
- ❏ A259. American Beauty Plaque
  from the Illusion series
- ❏ A260. American Beauty Spiral
  from the Illusion series

1994

- ❏ A261. New Life
- ❏ A262. English Garden
- ❏ A263. Sweet Summer—
  Second in the Four Seasons Bouquet series
- ❏ A264. Sweet Summer Plaque
  from the Illusion series
- ❏ A265. Walden Pond—
  Sixth in the Pond Life series
- ❏ A266. Fuchsia Frolic Plaque
  from the Illusion series
- ❏ A267. Spring Bouquet Rainbow
  from the Illusion series
- ❏ A268. American Beauty Egg
- ❏ A269. A Touch of Class Rosebush Triple
- ❏ A270. American Beauty Rosebush Triple
- ❏ A271. Breath of Life Plaque
  from the Illusion series
- ❏ A272. Breath of Life Rosebush Triple
- ❏ A273. The Quintessential Rosebush Triple
- ❏ A274. The Consummate Rosebush Triple
- ❏ A275. The Fabulous Rose Weight

1995

- ❏ A276. A Touch of Class—*Fifth in the Rose series*
- ❏ A277. Black Rose
- ❏ A278. Paradise —*Sixth in the Hummingbird series*
- ❏ A279. Enchantment
- ❏ A280. Symphony
- ❏ A281. Turtle & Dragonfly
- ❏ A282. On Golden Pond—
  Seventh in the Pond Life series
- ❏ A283. Misty Mornings—
  Third in the Four Seasons Bouquet series
- ❏ A284. Angelica *from the Illusion series*

- ❏ A285. Paradise Plaque *from the Illusion series*
- ❏ A286. In the Treetop *from the Emergence series*

1996

- ❏ A287. Ballerina—*Sixth in the Rose series*
- ❏ A288. Ballerina Pond Magnum
- ❏ A289. Ballerina Spiral *from the Illusion series*
- ❏ A290. Springtime in Mallorca
- ❏ A291. Passing Glory—
  Ninth in the Butterfly series
- ❏ A292. Blueberry Hill
- ❏ A293. Black-Throated Blue Warbler with Wild Columbines—*First in the Audubon series*
- ❏ A294. White Mountain Bouquet
- ❏ A295. Drink of Life—
  Seventh in the Hummingbird series
- ❏ A296. Anticipation—
  First in the Nature's Camouflage series
- ❏ A297. Midnight Blue *from the Glasscape series*
- ❏ A298. Bergunder Chrysanthemum
- ❏ A299. Stargazer Lily
- ❏ A300. Mother Nature
- ❏ A301. Misty Blue—*Seventh in the Rose series*
- ❏ A302. Caribbean Night
- ❏ A303. Pansy
- ❏ A304. Poinsettia
- ❏ A305. Rose Bud
  from the Denali Collaborations series
- ❏ A306. Lady's-Slipper Radiance
  from the Denali Collaborations series
- ❏ A307. Honeysuckle Radiance
  from the Denali Collaborations series
- ❏ A308. Flower Bud
  from the Denali Collaborations series

Items Missing from the Record

Photos of a few rare pieces were unavailable for photography as this book went to press. In an effort to present the most complete record possible, we include descriptions of these missing pieces in this section.

A20. WOODPECKER IN FLIGHT

A woodpecker is displayed in a flying pose. Produced in faceted and unfaceted crystal. Limited edition of 2.

A61. MALE & FEMALE HOUSE WREN

Ayotte records the striking differences between the male and female of the species. Limited edition of 50.

A142. MOCKINGBIRD WITH MAGNOLIA

A melodious mockingbird, State Bird of Mississippi, rests under a blushing pink magnolia. Limited edition of 75.

He is the king of song, often imitating other species for pure pleasure. The magnolia and the mockingbird together have a distinctly Southern feel.

A186. SOUTHERN MAGNOLIA WITH MOCKINGBIRD

A mockingbird inhales the fragrance of a large magnolia blossom. Limited edition of 50. Miniature—unlimited.

The mockingbird always reminds me of hazy summer nights spent down south among fragrant magnolias.

A250. MOCKINGBIRD WITH ORANGE BLOSSOMS

A mockingbird, the State Bird of Florida, perches in branches of delicate orange blossoms, the State Flower of Florida. One-of-a-kind.

Public Collections

The Art Institute of Chicago, Illinois

The Bergstrom-Mahler Museum, Neenah, Wisconsin

The Corning Museum of Glass, New York

The Currier Gallery of Art, Manchester, New Hampshire

The Royal Ontario Museum, Ontario, Canada

The Smithsonian Institution, Washington D. C.

Exhibitions

Songs Without Words, a traveling retrospective of Ayotte's work opened at the Union Bank of California in San Francisco in 1996. The exhibit will travel the world through 1998.

Regions of the Flame, Philabaum Galleries, 1997.

Texas Paperweight Celebration, MSC Forsyth Center Galleries, Texas A&M University, 1996.

The Art of the Paperweight—Challenging Tradition traveling exhibit 1993–1995.
  • The Art Museum of Santa Cruz County, California
  • Muscatine Art Center, Iowa
  • Jones Museum of Glass and Ceramics, Maine
  • Villa Terrace Museum of the Decorative Arts, Wisconsin
  • MSC Forsyth Center Galleries, Texas A&M University
  • Scone Palace, Scotland

Paperweight Show, Grovewood Gallery, Michigan, 1995.

Paperweights from the Henry Melville Fuller Collection, The Currier Gallery of Art, New Hampshire, 1993.

Masterpieces of American Glass, This traveling exhibit, containing pieces from The Corning Museum of Glass and The Toledo Museum of Art, traveled througout the Soviet Union in 1990.

Glass: State of the Art 1984, 12th Annual National Glass Invitational, Habatat Galleries.